W9-BGQ-248

How to Cook Like a Jewish Grandmother

How to Cook Like a Jewish Grandmother

By Marla Brooks

PELICAN PUBLISHING COMPANY
GRETNA 2007

Copyright © 2005
By Marla Brooks
All rights reserved

First printing, March 2005
Second printing, November 2007

The word "Pelican" and the depiction of a pelican are trademarks
of Pelican Publishing Company, Inc., and are registered in the
U.S. Patent and Trademark Office.

Library of Congress Cataloging-in-Publication Data

Brooks, Marla.
  How to cook like a Jewish grandmother / by Marla Brooks.
        p. cm.
  Includes index.
  ISBN 9781589802155 (pbk. : alk. paper)
1. Cookery, Jewish. I. Title.

TX724.B78 2005
641.5'676—dc22

                                            2004024423

Printed in the United States of America
Published by Pelican Publishing Company, Inc.
1000 Burmaster Street, Gretna, Louisiana 70053

This book is dedicated to the owners of Slobod's Delicatessens, my grandparents Henry and Lena Slobod and my cousins Jack and Aldean Slobod. Even though they aren't here anymore to cook those delicious meals I used to love as a child, they left behind a legacy of love, an appreciation of family, and hundreds of terrific recipes to remember them by.

Grandma and Grandpa

Jack and Aldean Slobod.

CONTENTS

Introduction

Our approach to cooking and eating has changed a great deal in recent years. We've become a more health-conscious society and try to eat right. It's grown increasingly difficult to process all the dietary data we're fed on a regular basis because we seem to be continually inundated with helpful information that will allow us to live well into our golden years. While seemingly overwhelming, trying to keep current is nothing new. Nearly a century ago, people were just as perplexed as we are today. The preface to *The Universal Cookbook,* written in 1913 by Helen Cramp, reads: "The lively and intense interest now displayed everywhere in the art of cookery, which is at once the most ancient and the most modern of arts, marks such an advance over the

Slobod's Delicatessen.

9

pioneer days of domestic science as only a teacher of that subject, or an experienced housekeeper who has kept step with the march of progress, can fully appreciate."

Let's face it. Cooking trends come and go, and it's nearly impossible to keep up. We live, we learn and, in spite of it all, we eat. Sure, it's in our best interest to try and maintain a healthy lifestyle but by forcing ourselves to eat right, we develop that all-too-common ailment: Comfort Food Deprivation. There's probably not a person alive who doesn't salivate at the recollection of a favorite childhood meal. Because we savor those childhood memories, family recipes handed down from generation to generation change very little over the years. We dream of feasting on food where taste, not caloric intake, is what counts.

One of the most important things to remember when using this book is that you don't have to be a Jewish grandmother to cook like one. In my opinion, the one word that defines any grandmother's cooking is "love." But in the case of a Jewish grandmother, love and food are synonymous. Nothing pleases a Jewish grandmother more than watching her family sit down to a wonderfully prepared meal and eating until they are ready to bust. In her mind, seeing the family pushing themselves away from the table barely able to move is a nonverbal confirmation of their love and devotion to her. Of course, this is a Jewish grandmother, and that's not quite enough: Several minutes later, after she's cleared the table and the family has slowly made their way to the sofa, loosened any clothing that is constricting their waistline, and are struggling to sit upright, she will sail into the room with a huge tray of fresh fruit and cookies. *Oy vey!*

Having been raised by my grandmother, Lena Slobod, I had many opportunities to watch her prepare a variety of wonderful meals. She never used a recipe or wrote anything down. I was well into my teens before I realized that a lot of people actually used cookbooks. There were one or two in the house, but seemingly they were there just for show. *The Universal Cookbook* must've been a wedding gift because, rather than being an integral part of her domestic life, Grandma called it a "dust catcher." In her way of cooking, it was always a pinch of this and a handful of that.

Shortly after her marriage to Henry in 1919, Lena was a housewife in Kansas City, Missouri, with a husband and two young children to feed. Then in 1937 the family uprooted themselves to join Henry's older brother, Harry, and his family in Philadelphia. Harry Slobod, or "Pop," as everyone called him, ran Slobod's Delicatessen at 46th and Walnut Streets. Harry had lots of takeout foods and a few tables for sit-down dining. Pop always boasted the biggest corned beef and pastrami sandwiches around, and the store was packed from 6 A.M. to midnight. Henry followed in his big brother's footsteps

Mom outside the family store in 1941.

and decided to try his luck with Slobod's, a grocery store and deli at 5501 Chancellor Street, just a few blocks down.

The stores served a mixed ethnic neighborhood, comprised of many European immigrants. Unlike Slobod's Delicatessen, Henry's store was mainly a grocery, but they cooked for their valued customers one day a week. Although my grandfather's store had no tables for eating in, there was always a huge group of people lining up outside the door waiting for him to put the "Freshly Cooked Corned Beef" sign in the window. Grandpa would haul the giant iron pots onto his huge stove in the back room and prepare the meat while on the other side of the kitchen Lena would be making huge tubs of potato salad, coleslaw, and other yummy offerings. Lena always made a double batch of her potato salad and coleslaw for Harry's place, and they would do the same with their chopped liver and herring. By 10 A.M., all the food would be sold out and there were never any leftovers.

There was no such thing as "Day Old" in either store. Fresh baked goods were delivered daily at 7 A.M. by an old man in a faded, red-paneled truck. He'd unload the delectable fresh bread, cakes, apple fritters, and doughnuts, and by noon they were always sold out. On Sundays, the family would take long drives to farm stands in the Pennsylvania countryside to buy fresh produce for the week. Quality was very important to the Slobod clan.

By 1947, Pop and family moved to southern California, and Henry and family again followed suit. Henry went to work at a large deli in a local department store for a couple of years and in the early 1950s bought the deli department at a local market.

By that time, Lena had me to raise, and hung up her professional apron, but the Slobod house was always the place to celebrate birthdays, anniversaries, and holidays with scrumptious meals. She continued that tradition until her death in 1982.

Grandma's love of food and feeding hungry relatives and friends must've rubbed off on me because from a very early age I'd be in the kitchen helping her out. She taught me to make her delicious chopped liver, cheese blintzes, and cold beet borscht early on. I still have her old heavy iron food grinder that attaches to the cutting board, her big wooden bowl, and her hand chopper for making chopped herring. Food processors weren't invented yet, but even if they were around, I'm sure she would have considered them nonsense.

As a young adult, I knew I had to start writing all these recipes down, so I spent a lot of time in Grandma's kitchen watching her cook and taking notes. Thankfully, she lived to the ripe old age of eighty-nine, which afforded me plenty of time to get her best dishes into recipe form. Then I realized that while my grandmother's recipes were wonderful, so were those of the other grandmothers I knew and I began collecting recipes from other family members and friends. My recipe file is now bulging with delectable offerings that need to be passed on to future generations.

Many of the recipes in the book came from the kitchen of Slobod's Delicatessen. Some came over on the boat and landed on Ellis Island with my grandmother and the other immigrant grannies that have contributed their best recipes to this book. A few were made up over the ensuing years by the generations that followed.

Our dining room table was always full at mealtime.

How To Cook Like A Jewish Grandmother is a book of recipes for those brave folks who want to defy fate and truly enjoy a good old-fashioned meal. It will not include sodium levels, dietary fiber information, carbohydrate counts, or any other nutritional guidelines needed to maintain a healthy lifestyle. Taste is all that counts in this tome. That's not to say that there might not be a few accidentally healthy or low-calorie offerings in the book, but they are not intentional. They just happen to taste good, too.

You don't have to be Jewish to cook like a Jewish grandmother, nor do you have to be Jewish to enjoy the recipes offered in this book. It's all about comfort food and plenty of it. The recipes embrace the tastes of the Old World and are topped off with a huge dollop of love.

How to Cook Like a Jewish Grandmother

BREAKFAST/BRUNCH

❧

Out-of-town company always meant brunch at our house.

"Breakfast is the most important meal of the day," my grandmother used to tell me when, as a teenager, I told her all I wanted was a glass of orange juice. There was no arguing with her because to a Jewish grandmother if no food passes the lips at those specific times of the day meant for eating (or any other opportune moment they can shove a morsel down your gullet), the world just might come to an end. We'd barter back and forth for a compromise. The bartering was merely a formality because in the end I knew she'd win. "Children are starving in Europe!" she'd exclaim. "Well, why don't you send them my breakfast and then they won't be so hungry?" I'd answer back. After about five minutes, I'd skulk over to the table and admit defeat.

When I was little, there was no fighting on weekends because that's when Grandpa made breakfast. I'd wake up to the smell of pancakes, waffles, or Canadian bacon and eggs wafting in from the kitchen. I'd sit up in bed, call out for my grandpa, and he'd magically appear to piggyback me into the kitchen. I can still remember sitting in the built-in kitchen nook, with the old radio sitting on the table, and listening to my grandparents chatting back and forth in Yiddish. I couldn't understand a word they were saying, but it didn't matter because I was too busy stuffing my face to care.

Often, especially when relatives were in town, Sunday brunch was a common occurrence. Grandma would weigh the dining room table down with delectable goodies and then we'd eat until we were ready to plotz. I don't remember much about my great-uncle Sam, except for the fact that after every meal at our house, he'd ask for a Bromo Seltzer™, down it in one or two gulps, give an earsplitting *grepps* (burp), and retire to the sofa a happy man.

Grandma would make so much to eat that cooking dinner that night was unnecessary. Ditto for breakfast or lunch the next day. Maybe it's my heritage, but to me there is nothing more comforting than opening the refrigerator and finding dishes full of leftovers that I can nibble on.

Grandma would be so proud.

One-Eyed Sandwiches

The word sandwich may be a bit misleading, as you don't put two slices of bread together to eat a one-eyed sandwich. It's a fried slice of bread with the middle cut out and an egg cracked into the hole. I've also heard this dish referred to as "Ox Eyes" or "Bull's Eyes." Call it what you will—it's a quick and delicious way to start the day.

> **1 tbsp. butter, margarine, or nonstick
> cooking spray**
> **2 slices bread**
> **2 eggs**
> **Salt and pepper to taste**
> **Maple syrup, jam, or honey (optional)**

In a frying pan, melt butter or margarine (or spritz pan with spray) over medium heat. Punch a hole in middle of each bread slice with small glass. Place bread in warmed pan, and then crack an egg into each hole. Fry until bread is golden brown on bottom then flip over and fry until other side is brown and egg is set in the middle. Season to taste. Remove from pan and serve with maple syrup, jam, or honey. Serves 2.

Old-Fashioned Bagels from Scratch

Believe it or not, long before you could walk into a Starbucks and buy a bagel to accompany your latte, they were actually made at home. Are they time-consuming? Yes. Are they worth the effort? You bet!

8 cups flour
1 tbsp. salt
1 tbsp. sugar
2 cakes of fresh yeast
2 cups lukewarm potato water*
¼ cup oil
4 eggs, slightly beaten
2 qt. boiling water
2 tbsp. sugar

Sift flour, salt, and 1 tablespoon sugar into large mixing bowl. Soften yeast in ⅓ cup potato water, then add to the dry ingredients. Pour oil into remaining potato water, then stir it into flour and yeast mixture. Add eggs and mix well until you have a big ball of dough.

Knead dough on floured surface for about 10 minutes. Since dough must be firm, add a little more flour if necessary. After kneading is complete, place dough in a greased bowl and cover with a towel. Let rise at room temperature until dough rises to the top of the bowl (about 1 hour). Then punch it down and remove from bowl. Knead again until dough is smooth and elastic.

Pinch off pieces of dough and roll in your hands until you have a rope about 6 inches long and about ¾-inch wide. Pinch the ends together so you have a doughnut shape.

Add 2 tablespoons sugar to boiling water and drop in bagels one at a time. Turn them over as they pop to the surface. Boil for about a minute on the second side, then remove from water to a greased cookie sheet. Bake at 450 degrees for about 10 to 15 minutes until crust is golden brown. Makes about 2 dozen bagels

*Potato water is just water in which peeled potatoes have been cooked. You can use plain water if you prefer, but the flavor of the bagel will not be as good.

Lox, Bagels, and Cream Cheese

Most non-Jewish folk probably consider this to be the ultimate Jewish meal.

6 bagels
8 oz. cream cheese*
½ lb. thinly sliced lox*
6 slices red onion, thinly sliced

Cut bagels in half and spread with cream cheese. Top with lox and onion. Serves 6.

*Some folks prefer more lox, some more cream cheese. Alter the portions to suit your taste.

Rusty's Pizza Bagels

Since pizza came to America back at the turn of the century from Italy, people have been trying to build a better pizza pie. While pizza bagels can't compare to the original pizza pie, they do make quite a good snack.

2 bagels, sliced
½ cup favorite pasta sauce
¼ cup shredded mozzarella cheese

Cut bagels in half and toast them until lightly browned. Spread each slice with pasta sauce and sprinkle on mozzarella cheese. Place on a cookie sheet and broil until cheese is bubbly and slightly browned, watching it carefully in the process. Cheese under a broiler has a tendency to go from underdone to burnt in the blink of an eye.

This is just the basic recipe. Don't limit yourself to just sauce and mozzarella cheese. Be creative! As with regular pizza, pile on the toppings. Serves 2.

Lox, Egg, and Onion Scramble

Aside from smoked whitefish and cream cheese on a kaiser roll, this is my favorite weekend breakfast. Because it's a dish fit for a Jewish Princess, it always tastes better if you can coax someone else to make it for you.

> **6 eggs**
> **⅓ cup milk or water**
> **Salt and pepper to taste**
> **1 tbsp. margarine or butter**
> **¼ medium onion, chopped**
> **3 oz. lox, roughly chopped**

In large bowl, beat eggs, milk (or water), and salt and pepper thoroughly. Set aside.

Heat butter or margarine in a skillet over medium heat and add onions. Cook until clear. Add egg mixture and lox. Scramble until eggs are set and to your liking. Serve with toasted bagels and sliced tomatoes. Serves 4.

Stanley's Tomato and Egg Pie

Being a writer, producer, director, lyricist, actor, and all-around very busy person, it is a wonder the late Stanley Ralph Ross had any time to cook at all. He said that breakfast was his favorite meal of the day, and this was his favorite breakfast.

> **2 tbsp. butter**
> **1 can (16 oz.) peeled tomatoes**
> **6 oz. fresh mushrooms**
> **Herbs and spices to your liking**
> **2 oz. freshly shredded Parmesan cheese**
> **3 eggs**
> **6 slices of your favorite cheese**

Melt butter over low flame in medium-sized frying pan. Pour tomatoes in the pan and simmer for a couple of minutes, and then add mushrooms. Sprinkle with spices. Add Parmesan cheese and simmer another couple of minutes.

Break eggs onto tomatoes, cover the pan, and simmer for another two minutes. Add strips of cheese in a crosshatch fashion, re-cover the pan, and simmer another two minutes. If prepared correctly, it will be about one-inch high. Serve with fresh fruit, bacon, and toast. Makes 1 to 2 servings.

Fried Salami and Eggs

When my grandfather made breakfast on Sunday mornings, this was one of his favorite recipes. He always served it with a big slice of raw onion on the side. As for me, I like using catsup as well.

4 slices salami
2 eggs
1 tbsp. butter, margarine, or nonstick
    cooking spray
Salt and pepper to taste

Cut salami into chunks. In a mixing bowl, lightly beat eggs. Melt butter in a frying pan over medium heat. Add salami to pan and sauté until lightly browned. Pour egg mixture over cooked salami and scramble on medium heat until the eggs are set to your liking. Flip over like a pancake and cook another minute or two. Season to taste. Serves 1.

Pancakes from Scratch

Why bother making pancakes from scratch when there are dozens of perfectly good mixes and batters on the market? Homemade always tastes better because it's made with love.

> 2 cups flour
> ½ tsp. salt
> 2 tsp. baking powder
> 1 tsp. sugar
> 1½ cups milk
> 2 eggs, beaten
> 2 tbsp. melted butter
> 1 tsp. oil to coat griddle

Mix and sift all dry ingredients, then add milk and eggs. Mix thoroughly and add melted butter.

Drop pancake batter by the spoonful onto heated, greased griddle or frying pan. When the pancakes start to bubble on top, flip over and cook until golden brown. Serve with your favorite pancake topping. Serves 2.

Leon's Pfannkuchen

Pfannkuchen literally means a big pancake. Leon has been making this Tulper clan breakfast favorite for as long as anyone can remember.

> 3 egg yolks
> 2 tbsp. matzo meal
> 3 egg whites
> ¼ stick butter

Beat egg yolks and then add matzo meal. In a separate bowl beat egg whites until firm and then gently blend into yolk mixture.

Melt butter in a frying pan and pour in egg mixture. Brown the bottom, then flip over and brown the other side. Serve with jelly or powdered sugar. Makes 1 BIG pancake.

Judy's Hungarian Pancakes (Palacsinta)

Simply put, Hungarian pancakes are crepes with a wonderfully delicious nut and honey filling.

3 eggs
1¼ cup flour
1 cup milk
½ cup cold water
1 tsp. sugar
Pinch of salt
1½ tbsp. sweet butter, melted

Combine all ingredients in electric blender. Blend until smooth. Set aside at least 1 hour.

Brush a 7- to 8-inch skillet with oil (any kind except olive oil) and heat over moderately high heat. Pour in 3 teaspoons of batter, quickly tilting pan to cover with a thin film. Sauté crepe about one minute until brown, turn, and bake other side about ½ a minute. Transfer to plate. Continue with rest of batter, stacking crepes with waxed paper between each one. Makes about 12 crepes.

NUT FILLING

1 cup chopped walnuts
Clear honey
Warm milk

Blend nuts with enough milk and honey to make a spreadable paste. Spread a little of the paste, to taste, over each crepe. Fold each crepe in half, and serve immediately.

You can also fill crepes with your favorite crepe filling. Serves 6.

Grandma's Cheese Blintzes

When it comes to cheese blintzes, there seems to be some controversy about whether or not to add raisins. The frozen variety doesn't come with raisins, and neither do the blintzes at our local delicatessens. But to me, a cheese blintz without raisins is like gefilte fish without horseradish.

> 1 pound dry cottage cheese or hoop
>   cheese
> 1 egg yolk
> 1 tbsp. melted butter
> 1 tbsp. sugar
> Pinch of salt
> ½ cup raisins

Combine all ingredients. Set aside.

BLINTZES

> 1 cup flour
> ½ tsp. salt
> 4 eggs
> 1 cup water or milk
> Butter
> Sour cream for garnish

Sift together flour and salt. Beat eggs, then add liquid and continue beating. Gradually add flour to egg mixture, stirring constantly until the batter is smooth and on the thin side.

Lightly grease 6-inch skillet or crepe pan with butter. Heat the skillet over medium-high heat. Pour about ½ cup of batter into skillet and swirl batter around to completely cover the bottom of the pan. Quickly pour out any excess batter.

Fry until blintz begins to blister and the edges curl away from the side of the skillet. Flip out of the pan onto a plate or dishtowel, using wax paper between each to avoid them sticking together. It's okay if the top of the blintz is slightly moist. Pan should be regreased about every three or four blintzes. When all blintzes are fried, place 1 tablespoon filling in the center of each blintz on the browned side. Raise bottom flap of dough to cover filling. Fold over each side so they meet in the middle, then roll up like a jelly roll. Serve with sour cream. Serves 6.

Blueberry Blintzes

For those who were raised on cheese blintzes, these sweet delights are a nice change of pace. The sweetness of the berries is wonderfully complemented by the tartness of the sour cream garnish.

> **2 cups blueberries**
> **2 tbsp. sugar**
> **2 tbsp. flour**

Mix berries, sugar, and flour in a bowl. Toss well and set aside.

BLINTZES

> **1 cup flour**
> **½ tsp. salt**
> **4 eggs**
> **1 cup water or milk**
> **Butter for frying**
> **Sour cream for garnish**

Sift together flour and salt in a small bowl. In a larger bowl, beat eggs, then add water (or milk) and continue beating. Gradually add sifted flour and salt to egg mixture, stirring constantly until batter is smooth, not lumpy. It should be thin.

Lightly grease a 6-inch skillet or crepe pan with butter. Heat the skillet over a medium-high heat. Pour about ½ cup of batter into the skillet and quickly swirl the batter around to completely cover the bottom of the pan, and pour out any excess batter.

Fry until the blintz begins to blister and the edges curl away from the side of the skillet. Flip out of the pan onto a dishtowel. Use wax paper between layers to keep blintzes from sticking together. Only one side of the blintz should be browned. It's okay if the top of the blintz is slightly moist. Repeat until all batter is used up. Pan should be regreased about every three or four blintzes.

When all blintzes are fried, place 1 tablespoon filling in the center of each blintz on the browned side. Raise the bottom flap of dough to cover filling. Fold over each side so they meet in the middle, then roll up like a jelly roll. Lightly fry blintzes in oil or butter, or place in casserole dish and bake at 425 degrees until lightly browned. Garnish with sour cream. Serves 6.

Grandma's Easy French Toast

French toast is probably no more French than French fries or French's™ mustard, but it is a filling and delicious way to start the day. When Grandpa took a weekend off from cooking, this was Grandma's specialty.

2 eggs, beaten
⅛ cup water
⅛ tsp. vanilla or almond extract (optional)
⅛ tsp. Cinnamon
2 slices thickly sliced egg bread*
1 tbsp. butter or margarine for frying
Powdered sugar

Beat eggs, water, vanilla, and cinnamon together in a flat dish. Place bread slices in mixture until fully soaked through on both sides.

Melt butter in frying pan or griddle over medium heat. Transfer bread slices to frying pan and fry until lightly browned on both sides (about 2 minutes per side). Place on plate and top with powdered sugar. Serve with maple syrup, jam or honey. Serves 2

*Thick slices of cinnamon raisin bread also work well.

Aldean's Knishes

A knish is similar to a baked won ton or pierogi. While there are many, many fillings for knishes, there are only two types of knish dough: yeast and plain pastry. Both are quite delicious, and it's just a matter of taste which one you'll like best. This is the plain pastry version.

2 cups all-purpose flour
1 tsp. baking powder
½ tsp. salt
2 eggs, beaten
1 tbsp. oil or schmaltz
2 tbsp. water
1 egg yolk diluted with 1 tbsp. water

Preheat oven to 350 degrees. Sift together all dry ingredients in a bowl. Make a well in the center and add eggs, oil, and water. Mix thoroughly until dough is formed.

Turn out dough onto a lightly floured surface and with a rolling pin roll out to about ⅛-inch in thickness. Cut into squares or rounds using a knife, cookie cutter, or a glass.

Fill each knish with 2 tablespoons filling (see following three recipes), then moisten edge of the dough with a little water. Fold over and pinch edges together to form a tight seal. Many people like to crimp edges with a fork. This is not only decorative, but ensures a strong bond. Brush the knish with diluted egg yolk. Place on well-greased cookie sheet and bake for about 25 minutes or until golden brown. Makes about 18 knishes.

Aldean's Favorite Knish Fillings

POTATO FILLING

½ cup chopped onion
3 tbsp. butter or margarine
1 cup mashed potatoes
1 egg
½ tsp. salt
¼ tsp. pepper

Sauté onions in butter until translucent, and transfer to a large bowl. Add potatoes, egg, salt, and pepper and mix until mixture is light and fluffy.

CHEESE FILLING

1½ cups diced onions
4 tbsp. butter
2 cups dry cottage cheese or hoop cheese
1 egg
Salt and pepper to taste
2 tbsp. sour cream

Sauté onions, then beat in remaining ingredients until smooth.

CHICKEN FILLING

1½ cups cooked ground chicken
¾ cup mashed potatoes
1 egg
1 tsp. salt
¼ tsp. pepper

Mix all ingredients until smooth.

Aldean's Knishes II

These knishes are made with yeast dough. Aside from taking time to let the dough rise, they are no more difficult to make than their pastry dough cousins.

1 tbsp. sugar
¾ cup lukewarm water
½ tsp. salt
¼ cup salad oil or schmaltz
1 cake of yeast
2 eggs slightly beaten
¾ cups flour

Dissolve sugar in water, add salt, schmaltz, and yeast. Let stand until yeast is softened, about 5 minutes. Stir in eggs, then flour, blending in the flour a little at a time to make a soft dough. Turn dough out on a lightly floured board and knead until smooth and elastic. Add more flour as needed. Place dough in a greased bowl, cover with a dishtowel, and allow to rise in a warm place until it doubles in size (about 1 hour).

Punch down dough and remove from bowl. Roll out very thinly on a lightly floured board until you have a rectangle of about 15-by-24 inches. Brush dough with melted fat or oil and place a row of filling (about 1 cup) 1 inch from the edge of dough, then roll up like a jelly roll (about 3 turns). Cut the roll into 1-inch pieces. Stretch dough up and over edges of each piece to seal in the filling.

Brush knishes with melted fat and place on greased cookie sheet, about ¾-inch apart. Let rise for about 30 minutes, then bake in a 375-degree oven for about 25 minutes, or until knishes are golden brown. Makes about 8 dozen knishes.

EASY BEEF AND POTATO FILLING

2 cups chopped onion
2 tbsp. shortening
2½ cups mashed potatoes
1 tbsp. salt
¼ tsp. pepper
5 cups sautéed ground beef
1 egg

Sauté onions in shortening until translucent, then add remaining ingredients and blend well. Makes about 6 cups.

Rusty's Chicken Wings

When it comes to cooking, my mother's method was to make it taste good and get it done fast. These delicious wings prove that you don't have to have dozens of ingredients to end up with a tasty finger food.

16 chicken wings
1 tsp. garlic powder
Honey

Preheat oven to 350 degrees. Lay out wings in a single layer on a cookie sheet. Sprinkle with garlic powder and drizzle with honey. Bake at 350 degrees for 1 hour or until skin is brown and crispy. Serves 4.

Judy's Chopped Chicken Liver

There are as many versions of chopped chicken liver as there are cooks that make it. Judy's parents were Hungarian, hence the addition of paprika.

1 lb. chicken livers
2 tbsp. chicken fat or butter
2 hard-boiled eggs
1 small onion
4 sprigs parsley
1 tsp. salt
½ tsp. paprika

Rinse chicken livers with cold water and drain on absorbent paper. Melt chicken fat (or butter) in skillet over low heat. Add livers, turning occasionally, and cook 5 to 10 minutes, or until lightly browned. Remove from heat and set aside until livers are cool.

Finely chop chicken livers, eggs, onion, and parsley. Mix ingredients together in a bowl. Chill in refrigerator for about 4 hours to allow flavors to blend. Serve with crisp, dry toast. Makes 10 to 12 servings.

Grandma's Sweet and Sour Meatballs

Grandma's meatballs were a family favorite, and she made them often. She usually served them as an appetizer, but they're also quite good as a main dish served with boiled potatoes or rice on the side to sop up the gravy.

> **1 lb. ground beef**
> **1 onion, finely chopped**
> **1 tbsp. breadcrumbs**
> **1 egg**
> **1 tsp. salt**
> **Pepper to taste**
> **1 tbsp. schmaltz or shortening**
> **2 cups hot water**
> **1 lemon, thinly sliced and seeded**
> **1/4 cup sugar**
> **1/4 cup raisins**

Mix together beef, onion, breadcrumbs, egg, salt, and pepper. Form the mixture into balls (any size you choose will work).

In a Dutch oven or heavy skillet, brown meatballs in shortening. Then add water, lemons, sugar, and raisins. Bring to a boil, then cover and reduce heat and simmer for about 45 minutes. Serves 4 to 6.

Judy's Sweet and Sour Meatballs

As with most Jewish recipes, there are many versions of sweet and sour meatballs. Instead of boiling the meatballs in a broth, this recipe calls for baking them first and then adding them to the sauce.

> **2 lb. ground meat**
> **½ cup breadcrumbs**
> **½ cup catsup**
> **2 eggs**
> **1½ tsp. garlic or seasoned salt**

Mix all ingredients together. Using a measuring teaspoon as a guide, form small meatballs, then place them in shallow baking pan and bake in a 500-degree oven for 10 minutes. While meatballs are baking, make the sauce.

SAUCE

> **¼ cup chicken broth**
> **¼ cup brown sugar**
> **¾ cup vinegar**
> **1 tbsp. soy sauce**
> **1 tbsp. catsup**
> **4 tbsp. cornstarch**
> **1 green pepper (sliced)**
> **1 red onion (sliced)**
> **2 cans (14 oz. each) chunk pineapple,**
> **drained**

Blend all ingredients except for pineapple, green pepper, and red onion; cook sauce until it thickens. Let cool, and then add green pepper and red onion. Add pineapple chunks and meatballs to the sauce. Place all in fondue pot or chafing dish to serve. Serves 6 to 8.

Carrie's Matzo Pizza

While Carrie's version of the classic pizza is unique, it's very tasty, a great finger food, and a wonderful way to use up all that leftover Passover matzo.

> 2 matzos
> 1 can (6 oz.) tomato paste
> ¼ lb. cooked ground beef
> ¼ lb. mozzarella, cheddar, or provolone
>   cheese, shredded

Spread matzo with a layer of tomato paste. Top with ground beef and cheese. Bake in a 400-degree oven until cheese melts. Serves 2.

Judy's Broccoli Corn Bread

Plain old corn bread recipes leave themselves wide open for experimentation. Jalapeño corn bread, for instance, has been recently making a name for itself among gourmets. Judy's broccoli corn bread is for those with a more sensitive palate.

> 1 package (10 oz.) chopped broccoli,
>   cooked and drained
> 1 stick margarine, melted
> 4 eggs, beaten
> 1 large onion, chopped
> ¾ tsp. salt
> 6 oz. sour cream
> 1 package of your favorite corn bread
>   mix

Mix all ingredients. Pour into 8½-by-11-inch greased pan and bake at 350 degrees until set. Serves 4 to 6.

APPETIZERS

No meal could begin without the requisite schnapps and a toast.

Classically, an appetizer is a small portion of food or drink served as the first course of a meal to stimulate the appetite. An aperitif is an alcoholic beverage served before the meal for the same purpose. No meal in the Slobod household, with the possible exception of breakfast, was ever served without both. While Grandma was putting out the appetizers, Grandpa would pour each adult male a shot glass of schnapps. The women and children usually made due with a glass of tomato juice or ginger ale.

On holidays, though, everyone got the requisite glass of Manischewitz® wine. To the uninitiated, this thick, sweet wine is not unlike cough syrup. To a child, it's like ambrosia. Several family members chose to make their own crude wine coolers, by adding a little seltzer to the glass. It seems that watering it down made it easier to get down.

After the wine came plate after plate of pre-dinner "noshes." There was always a crudités plate of fresh vegetables, another with kosher dill pickles and other pickled vegetables, and ripe black olives as well. When Grandma felt "creative," she'd also throw in a few green olives for good measure. While many of the types of vegetables offered varied with the season, there was always a plate of sliced raw onions for Grandpa. He couldn't eat a meal without them.

There were usually so many tempting appetizers put out, one could have easily made a meal on those alone, but we had to use restraint because God forbid we didn't save room for the rest of the meal.

Garlicky Marinated Mushrooms

Mushrooms are great because they soak up flavor like a sponge. When you cook them slightly in a hot marinade, the flavor is immediately infused.

1 lb. fresh whole mushrooms
¼ cup vinegar
¾ cup oil
6 garlic cloves, diced
1 tbsp. finely diced onion
¼ tsp. dry mustard
Salt and pepper to taste

Clean mushrooms and set aside. Mix remaining ingredients in saucepan and bring to a boil. Reduce heat, add mushrooms, and let simmer for about 5 minutes. Remove from heat, place in bowl, and cover. Refrigerate and let marinate for at least 24 hours before serving. Serves 4 to 6.

Tangy Pickled Vegetables

These are great to keep in the refrigerator for a quick nosh, or as an accompaniment to a meal.

1 large cucumber, peeled and sliced
2 small zucchini, sliced
½ lb. mushrooms, cut in half
1 large onion, sliced in rings
1 cup vinegar
1 cup water
2 tsp. salt
4 tbsp. sugar

Prepare vegetables and place in large bowl. Add vinegar, water, salt, and sugar to a saucepan and bring to a boil. Pour over vegetables and toss well. Refrigerate for at least 2 hours before serving, tossing the mixture once or twice during that time to marinate evenly. Serves 4 to 6.

Pickled Green Tomatoes

We usually eat pickled tomatoes as a condiment, but they can also be sliced and breaded in flour or corn meal and fried as a side dish, just like those famous fried green tomatoes served in the South. The only difference is that these are, with apologies to Emeril, "kicked up a notch."

> **24 green tomatoes**
> **½ cup salt**
> **2 qt. water**
> **1 cup vinegar**
> **6 cloves garlic**
> **2 bay leaves**
> **15 whole peppercorns**
> **1½ tsp. pickling spices**
> **3 tbsp. dried dill**

Wash tomatoes well and place in a large jar or crock. Bring remaining ingredients to a boil, then set aside to cool for a few minutes. Pour over tomatoes, making sure all are covered. Seal jar and keep in a cool place (do not refrigerate. It is fine to leave the jar on the kitchen counter, but away from the stove) for about a week.

The tomatoes can be pickled either whole or cut in half, but keep in mind that the halves will require less pickling time. Makes 24 servings.

Slobod's Deli Dill Pickles

At Slobod's Deli, the pickle barrel stood right beside the crock of pickled eggs.

25 pickling cucumbers
½ cup kosher salt
2 qt. water
2 tbsp. white vinegar
6 cloves garlic
3 bay leaves
1½ tsp. pickling spices
10 sprigs fresh dill

Carefully wash and dry cucumbers and place them in a large crock or jar. Combine remaining ingredients and bring to a boil, cool, and then pour over cucumbers. Seal the crock and store in a cool place (do not refrigerate. It is fine to leave the jar on the kitchen counter, but away from the stove) for about a week. If you like "half done" pickles, you can test for taste in about 4 days. Makes 25 pickles.

Dill Pickle Canoes

These quick-to-make appetizers are a great little treat. While purists might opt for using plain cream cheese, any of the savory varieties available at the store will work. I'm rather partial to pimiento, myself.

Large dill pickles
Whipped cream cheese

Slice each pickle in half lengthwise and carefully scoop out centers with a small spoon or melon baller. Stuff with cream cheese. Serves as many as you like!

Picklelilies

These incredibly simple finger food appetizers are so named because of their resemblance to a lily flower. Personally, I think they look more like a pickle in a blanket.

1 lb. thinly sliced salami
1 jar sweet pickles (whole pickles, not the
sweet pickle chips)

Wrap each pickle lengthwise with a slice of salami; secure with a toothpick. Serves as many as you like!

Dilly Pickled Eggs

A big crock of pickled eggs was always on the counter at Slobod's Deli. Grandpa used to eat them as a snack with a big fat soft pretzel and a mug of beer.

3 cups white vinegar
1½ cups water
1 tsp. salt
1 tsp. whole peppercorns
2 cloves of garlic, smashed
1 tsp. dried dill or 2 tsp. fresh dill
2 tsp. pickling spice
12 hard boiled eggs, peeled

Combine all ingredients except for eggs in a saucepan and bring to a boil. Lower heat and let simmer for 15 minutes. Cool.

Place eggs in a clean, sterilized jar and pour in vinegar mixture to completely cover eggs. For a real kick, try adding a teaspoon or two of red pepper flakes. Seal tightly (no need to refrigerate—the vinegar is a preservative). Depending on how tangy you want your eggs, don't open the jar for at least two weeks for a mild flavor and up to a month for a stronger flavor. Makes 12 servings.

Grandma's Devilishly Good Deviled Eggs

This was Grandma's catchall recipe. She also made her egg salad, tuna salad, and salmon salad with the same basic ingredients.

6 hard-boiled eggs
2 tbsp. mayonnaise
1 tbsp. sweet pickle relish
Salt and pepper to taste
Paprika

Cut each egg in half lengthwise and remove the yolks to a mixing bowl. Add mayonnaise, pickle relish, and salt and pepper and mash together until smooth. Fill the hollowed-out egg whites with the mixture. Top with a sprinkle of paprika. Makes 12 servings.

"Something's Fishy" Deviled Eggs

If you are the adventurous sort and don't have to worry about your salt intake, you can substitute anchovies in this recipe for the noble sardine.

6 hard-boiled eggs
2 tbsp. mayonnaise
1 tsp. prepared mustard
1 tsp. minced onion
4 oz. skinless, boneless sardines, mashed
Salt and pepper to taste
Parsley for garnish

Cut each egg in half lengthwise and remove the yolks to a mixing bowl. Combine with the rest of the ingredients and mash all together until smooth. Fill the hollowed-out egg whites with the mixture. Garnish with parsley. Makes 12 servings.

Slobod's Tuna "Horsey Doovers"

Nothing is simpler than tuna salad, and when placed on a melba round with a bit of melted cheese on top, you've got a lovely little appetizer.

>1 can (12 oz.) tuna
>¼ cup mayonnaise
>1 stalk celery, chopped
>¼ cup chopped onion
>2 tbsp. sweet pickle relish
>¼ tsp. rosemary
>1 box garlic Melba toast rounds or other
>   hard, dense cracker
>½ cup shredded cheddar cheese

Mix together all ingredients, except cheese and crackers. Blend well. Place teaspoonful of tuna mixture on cracker and top with a bit of shredded cheese. You can either place these under the broiler or in the microwave to heat and melt the cheese. Serve immediately. Makes about 2 dozen hors d'oeuvres.

Grandma's Old-Fashioned Gefilte Fish

Yes, you're right—making gefilte fish from scratch is a chore. But there is nothing like homemade.

>3 lb. whitefish, carp, or yellow pike
>   (whichever fish you choose, make sure to
>   keep the head, bones, and skin for broth)
>2 eggs
>½ cup cold water
>3 tbsp. matzo meal or cracker crumbs
>Salt and pepper to taste
>2 medium onions
>3 carrots, sliced

Lightly salt the fish fillets and chill for 3 to 4 hours. Rinse and put fish fillets into a food processor or food grinder and process to a fine consistency.

Transfer fish to a large bowl and mix in eggs one at a time, water, matzo meal or crackers, and salt and pepper. Blend all together into a paste and set aside to chill in refrigerator for about 15 minutes.

Meanwhile, make broth by placing fish heads and bones into the bottom of a large Dutch oven. Slice onions and carrots and arrange over the bones. Add salt and pepper to taste, then cover with cold water and bring to a boil. Simmer for about five minutes.

Remove fish mixture from refrigerator and shape into balls of desired size.

Bring broth back up to a boil and place fish balls into boiling broth. Add sliced carrots and onions. Bring to a boil again, then cover and simmer gently on low heat for about 1 hour. Check pot every so often to make sure liquid hasn't evaporated. Add a little more if needed.

At end of cooking time, cool slightly before removing fish to a platter. Gefilte fish can be served hot or cold. Garnish with carrot and onion slices and broth. If you serve this cold, the broth will be jellied. Serve with horseradish, matzo, and green onions. Serves 6 to 8.

Mashed Sardine Spread

I used to wonder why Jewish folks loved their sardines until I found out that these little saltwater fish are members of the herring family. Then it made perfect sense. Actually, sardines are not one particular fish. Named after the island of Sardinia in the Mediterranean where the canning industry began, sardines include Pacific, Atlantic, and blueblack herring as well as sprat and pilchard.

**1 slice egg bread
2 tbsp. vinegar
8½ oz. skinless, boneless sardines
1 hard-boiled egg
1 small onion, grated
½ tsp. sugar
Salt to taste**

Soak the bread in the vinegar to soften, and then combine the rest of the ingredients with the bread and mash with a fork until fine. Serve with either crackers or cocktail rounds. Serves 4 to 6.

Aldean's Chopped Herring

At the deli, Aldean made her chopped herring the old-fashioned way, using fresh fish that was chopped by hand. In later years, she'd occasionally start with ready-made pickled herring in a jar with surprisingly good results.

1 jar (32 oz.) herring in wine sauce
1 large onion, cut into quarters

Place herring and onion in food processor and grind until it reaches a fine consistency. Serve on crackers or rye bread. Serves 6 to 8.

Rusty's Caviar

It was a New Year's tradition for Mom to make her "doctored-up" caviar. If you're squeamish about having a lot of fish eggs in your mouth, just pretend they are very salty poppy seeds.

1 jar (2 oz.) black caviar
1 hard-boiled egg, thinly sliced
1 tbsp. finely chopped green onion
Black pepper to taste
1 box round unsalted water crackers

Place caviar in small bowl. Take one of the ends of the egg that doesn't contain yolk and mash it up with a fork. Mix into caviar along with onions and a dash of black pepper. Gently blend well, taking care to not mash or crush the caviar.

If possible, make the caviar 2 hours before serving to allow flavors to blend, but don't spoon onto crackers until immediately before serving. To serve, put a dollop of mixture on a cracker that has been topped with a thin slice of egg. Serves 4 to 6.

Slobod's Deli Chopped Liver

The consistency of the liver will depend on the method used to grind it. In the deli and at home, Grandma used one of those hand-crank food grinders. I usually use a food processor, but use the pulse button to keep the consistency from becoming too fine. Chopped liver needs to have a little substance. Even though they are quite similar, you don't want to whip your liver into a creamy pâté.

> **2 lb. chicken livers**
> **2 tbsp. schmaltz (chicken fat) or Rokeach**
> **Nyafat™ (a schmaltz substitute found**
> **in the kosher section of most markets)**
> **1 large onion, sliced**
> **2 hard-boiled eggs**
> **6 saltine crackers, crushed**
> **Salt and pepper to taste**

Clean and rinse livers, picking off as many of those little yellow globules as possible. They make the liver bitter if left on. In large skillet, sauté onions in shortening over medium heat until brown. Add liver and sauté until thoroughly cooked, about 5 minutes. Remove from heat and let cool for about 5 minutes. Transfer liver and onions, eggs, and cracker crumbs to food processor and pulse until thoroughly mixed. If mixture is too dry, add a little more schmaltz. Spread on crackers, matzo, or rye bread with a little extra raw onion on top. Serves 6 to 8.

Leftover Tongue Spread

Because I used to watch in horror as my grandmother boiled and peeled those huge cow tongues when I was very little, the idea of eating it in its original form doesn't exactly appeal to me. Grinding and seasoning it beyond recognition makes this dish more aesthetically palatable.

> **3 cups ground smoked beef tongue**
> **½ medium onion, finely chopped**
> **⅓ cup mayonnaise**
> **¼ sweet pickle relish**
> **Salt and pepper to taste**

Mix all ingredients in a bowl until well-blended. Serve on rye bread or crackers. Serves 6 to 8.

Kosher Pigs in Blankets

I suppose this is the kosher version of an old favorite. They're easy to make for a quick meal or snack. Served with a tossed salad, or coleslaw, these little piggies make a great meal. If you don't like crescent rolls, experiment with other types of frozen bread dough.

> **1 package of refrigerated crescent roll**
> **dough**
> **8 kosher hot dogs**

Lay out crescent rolls. Place a hot dog at the wide end of each piece of dough and roll up around the hot dog. Bake according to package directions on the dough. Serve with catsup, mustard, or barbecue sauce. Serves 4.

SOUPS AND STEWS

❧

Harry and Henry Slobod, owners of the two Slobod's Delicatessens, were men who loved their soup "stove-hot."

We had soup almost every day, and nobody could eat soup as hot as my grandfather, with the possible exception of the late George Burns. When I was working on my first celebrity cookbook and asked Burns for a recipe, he replied by saying that, while he himself didn't cook, if the soup was "stove-hot" and there was a bottle of catsup on the table, he was a happy man. In Grandpa's case, all it took was stove-hot soup and sliced raw onion. I guess the moral of the story is: Never serve a Jewish man lukewarm soup.

In spite of the fact that it was always on the household menu, I was never really enthralled with soup. As a rule, I didn't eat any if I could get away with it. But, as rules are made to be broken, there were a couple of exceptions. These were soups that were the meal, rather than being just a part of it, and those I enjoyed with great pleasure. They are seasonal offerings: one for the dead of winter (or at least the winter months because in California our winters are never very cold compared to other parts of the country) and the other for stifling summer days when it is just too hot to eat anything but cold food.

The winter soup, hot cabbage borscht, filled my grandmother's house with a delicious aroma. The combination of meat, cabbage, lemon juice, and brown sugar makes it a sweet and sour delight. This was one of Grandma's favorites as well. She used to say that it reminded her of her childhood in Russia. To this day, it always reminds me of my childhood as well. It's one of my favorite comfort foods.

Having cold beet borscht for a summer meal is like swallowing a magical tonic that immediately cools the body down. It's light, refreshing, and another childhood meal that I continue to make on a regular basis. It's been my experience that non-Jewish men aren't too crazy about beets, and will usually do a double take when seeing a bowl of this borscht for the first time because of it's Pepto-Bismol™-like hue. They don't know what they are missing.

Whether your preference is for hot or cold soup, the following recipes should stand you in good stead.

Slobod's Deli Hot Cabbage Borscht

There is nothing better than a steaming bowl of hot cabbage borscht with a slice of pumpernickel bread on a cold winter day. It not only nourishes the body, but warms the soul as well. This is one of those comfort foods of my childhood that I absolutely cannot live without. Grandma would use the same broth to boil her stuffed cabbage, with delicious results.

> **2 lb. short ribs**
> **1½ qt. water**
> **1 onion, diced**
> **2 cups canned tomatoes**
> **1 small head cabbage, shredded**
> **Juice of 2 lemons**
> **¼ cup brown sugar**
> **2 tsp. salt**
> **Pepper to taste**

Bring meat to a rapid boil in water. Skim off scum; add onion and tomatoes. Bring again to a boil, lower heat, and simmer for about 2 hours.

Add cabbage to the borscht, cover, and simmer another 30 minutes. Add the lemon juice, brown sugar, salt, and pepper. Simmer about 10 minutes more, taste, and adjust seasonings.

The amounts of lemon juice and brown sugar in this sweet and sour soup will vary according to taste. Some prefer it sweeter and others like it more on the tart side. Start with the amounts listed above and then add more of one or the other to suit your taste. Serves 8.

Grandma's Hot Beef Borscht (Fleishig Borscht)

Somehow this borscht tastes better with fresh beets, not canned. Its sweet and sour flavor is similar to that of hot cabbage borscht.

2 qt. water
2 lb. beef brisket
10 small beets, julienned or diced
2 yellow onions, sliced
Juice of 2 lemons
2 tbsp. sugar
2 tsp. salt
Pepper to taste

Place the water, meat, beets, and onions in a Dutch oven and bring to a boil. Then lower heat to simmer and cook until the meat is tender. Add lemon juice, sugar, salt, and pepper and simmer about 10 minutes. Taste for seasonings. Serve with either oyster crackers or broken up matzo as a garnish. Serves 6 to 8.

Slobod's Vegetable Soup

As I mentioned before, Grandpa loved his soup and most meals began with a hot, steamy bowl. As Grandma tried to cook healthy meals, this savory soup made with fresh vegetables really fit the bill.

½ cup chopped onion
1 tbsp. butter or margarine
2 cups red cabbage, shredded
½ cup chopped carrots
1 leek, cleaned
1 tbsp. chopped green pepper
1½ tsp. salt
Pepper to taste
1 tomato, diced
1 tbsp. chopped celery
1 clove garlic, diced
1½ qt. water
1 cup diced potato
2 zucchini, sliced

Brown onion in butter or margarine. Add all vegetables, except potato and zucchini. Add water, cover pot, and simmer for about 45 minutes. Add potato and zucchini and simmer covered for another 15 minutes. Serves 4 to 6.

Cream of Spinach Soup

Spinach is high in iron and low in calories. Add a little onion and a bit of cream, and you've got the makings for a quick, delicious soup.

> 1 qt. fresh spinach
> ½ tbsp. chopped onion
> 1 pint cream
> Salt and pepper to taste

Wash spinach carefully, then place in a dry Dutch oven and stir over medium heat until wilted. Drain spinach, reserving any water. Chop finely and return to water. Add onion and cook until thoroughly done. You may need to add a bit more water during the cooking process.

Place onion and cooked spinach in a blender and add cream. Season well. Blend until smooth. Serves 4.

Creamy Celery Soup

Even though we live in an age where "hot and spicy" is the taste du jour, this savory and creamy soup is great for those who have a more delicate palate.

> 1 celery root, peeled and diced
> ½ lb. potatoes, peeled and thickly sliced
> 2 tbsp. butter or margarine
> 3 cups water
> 1 can (16 oz.) chicken broth
> 1 tbsp. flour
> Salt and pepper to taste
> 4 tbsp. sour cream

Sauté celery root and potatoes in half the butter, then add water, chicken broth, flour, and salt and pepper. Bring to a boil, cover and simmer for about 45 minutes, then stir in sour cream and remaining butter. Let cool, then transfer mixture to a blender and blend well. You may need to add a bit more broth if you prefer a more liquid consistency. Serve hot, garnished with croutons. Serves 4 to 6.

Creamy Fresh Corn Soup

There's nothing better than cooking with fresh ingredients, and using fresh corn is really no harder than opening up a can. Because the corncobs themselves are used in this recipe for flavoring, don't make this soup unless you're planning to use fresh corn.

3 ears sweet corn
Water to cover
1 bay leaf
Salt and pepper to taste
1 pint cream

Remove kernels from corncob, leaving husk on cob. Set aside. Break cobs in half and place in a kettle with enough water to cover. Boil cobs for about 20 minutes, then strain the liquid. Return liquid to the fire and bring to a boil. Add corn kernels, bay leaf, and salt and pepper to taste. Simmer for about 15 minutes and then add cream. Mix well and serve piping hot. Makes 4 servings.

Yummy Lentil Soup

A lentil is a member of the legume family with a wonderfully unique, nutty flavor. They are most commonly used in soups or salads.

1½ cups lentils, washed and drained
2 qt. water
1 onion, chopped
2 carrots, peeled and sliced
2 stalks celery, diced
2 tsp. salt
1 tsp. garlic powder
Salt and pepper to taste

Soak lentils overnight in cold water. Drain and add lentils and vegetables to water in Dutch oven or stewpot. Add seasonings. Bring to a boil, then reduce heat and simmer about 1½ hours or until lentils are tender. Adjust seasonings.

Some people will serve this soup country style as is, or you can put the soup into a blender to make it smooth and creamy. Serves 4 to 6.

Mom's Barley and Mushroom Soup

My mother loved barley, a starchy grain and one of the earliest plants known to man. It lends itself well as a breakfast cereal or as a soup and casserole ingredient.

½ lb. dry barley
½ lb. chopped mushrooms
1 small onion, diced
½ lb. cooked beef, sliced
¼ tsp. garlic powder
Salt and pepper to taste

Cook barley according to package directions. When barley is about three-quarters done, add mushrooms, onion, and cooked beef. Season with garlic powder, salt, and pepper. Cover and simmer on low heat for about half an hour. Serve hot. Serves 4.

Grandpa's Oxtail Soup

This is another one of those old-world soups that isn't high on everyone's favorite soup list. While Grandpa didn't make it very often, it was one of his favorites.

1 onion, chopped
½ tbsp. shortening
1 oxtail, cut into pieces and separated at
   the joints
2 qt. cold water
2 whole cloves
2 peppercorns
Salt and pepper to taste
1 stalk celery, chopped
2 cloves garlic
1 bunch parsley, finely chopped

In small frying pan, brown onion in shortening. While browning, place meat and water in large Dutch oven or stewpot. When it comes to a boil, add onion, spices, celery, garlic, and parsley. Simmer over low heat for about 4 hours. Then strain and cool. Remove grease. Reheat, adjust seasonings, and serve hot. Serves 4.

Grandpa's P'cha

I don't remember this calf's foot soup ever being served in my lifetime but, according to my mother, it was another of Grandpa's favorites when she was growing up. The broth turns into a jelly when you refrigerate it, but liquefies when you reheat it, which is how my grandmother served it.

> **2 calves' feet, chopped into 2-inch pieces**
> **1 tsp. salt**
> **½ tsp. ground black pepper**
> **1 onion, quartered**
> **3 qt. cold water**
> **3 cloves crushed garlic**
> **2 celery stalks with tops**
> **2 sprigs fresh dill or 1 tsp. dried dill weed**
> **2 sprigs parsley**

Make sure calves' feet are washed thoroughly. Then add feet, salt, pepper, and onion to cold water and bring to a boil. Reduce heat, cover, and simmer for about 2 hours.

Toss out bones, but save marrow and cartilage. Strain broth and then add garlic and marrow. Chop cartilage and add to pot. Refrigerate for about 4 hours or until mixture jells. Skim fat and reheat broth. Add celery, dill, and parsley and bring to a boil, then cover and simmer for another 30 minutes or so. Before serving, remove celery, parsley, and dill. Serves 6.

Easy Beef Stew

One pot meals are terrific when you're on a tight schedule and don't have the time to slave over a hot stove. This is one of those yummy meals where you just need to throw everything into the pot and go about your business.

> 1 lb. stew beef or chuck
> 2 tsp. oil
> 1 small onion, chopped
> 2 cloves garlic, mashed
> 1 large potato, cubed
> 2 carrots, peeled and sliced
> 1 can (16 oz.) stewed tomatoes
> ½ tsp. oregano
> 1 bay leaf
> 1 tsp. Worcestershire sauce
> Dash of hot sauce (optional)
> Salt and pepper to taste

Brown meat and onion in oil in a Dutch oven. Add garlic, potato, carrots, tomatoes, and remaining ingredients. Bring to a boil, then cover and simmer over low heat for about 2 hours, or until meat is tender. Serves 4.

Grandma's Chili Con Carne

This is one of those recipes that is an Americanized version of the classic Mexican dish.

> **2 lb. ground beef**
> **1 small onion, chopped**
> **1 can (40 oz.) pinto beans**
> **2 cans (16 oz. each) diced tomatoes**
> **1 whole pickled jalapeno pepper**
>   **(optional)**
> **1 tbsp. chili powder**
> **1 tsp. oregano**
> **1 tsp. garlic powder**
> **Hot sauce to taste**
> **Salt and pepper to taste**

Brown ground beef and onion in a Dutch oven. Drain off fat. Add remaining ingredients and bring to a boil. Cover and simmer about 1 hour to allow flavors to blend. Serves 6 to 8.

Slobod's Deli Chicken Soup

The best thing about making chicken soup (a.k.a. Jewish penicillin) is the way it fills the house with a delectable aroma. Another plus is that you can add so many different things to it, depending on what you have on hand.

> 1 chicken (4 to 5 lb.), cut up
> 3 qt. water
> 1 tbsp. salt
> 1 onion, quartered
> 2 carrots, peeled and sliced
> 4 celery tops or ½ tsp. celery seed
> 1 tsp. poultry seasoning
> 1 or 2 bay leaves
> ½ tsp. poultry seasoning
> Salt and pepper to taste

Wash chicken and place in salted water in stew pot or Dutch oven. Bring to a boil and then skim off scum. Add remaining ingredients and then simmer until chicken is tender. Remove chicken and strain soup. Place soup in refrigerator to cool and allow fat to rise to surface and congeal. Remove fat before reheating.

Add noodles, cooked rice, matzo balls, potato dumplings, chicken meat, or kreplach before serving. Serves 8.

Potato Dumplings for Soup (Knaidlach)

Potato dumplings are a nice change from matzo balls and not hard to make. As with matzo balls, some people like their dumplings soft, others like them as dense as bowling balls. This recipe makes a light, fluffy dumpling.

> 1 cup mashed potatoes, freshly made
> ½ cup hot water or broth
> 3 tbsp. shortening
> Salt and pepper to taste
> 3 eggs, beaten
> 1 cup matzo meal
> Previously prepared chicken broth

Add hot liquid to mashed potatoes and mix until smooth. Add shortening, salt and pepper to taste, and mix well. Lightly fold eggs and matzo meal into the mixture, then chill for 3 to 4 hours.

Roll mixture into small balls and drop gently into previously prepared chicken broth. Cover and cook on low heat for about 15 to 20 minutes. Makes about 24 knaidlach.

Grandma's Cold Beet Borscht

This is an exceptionally refreshing dish on a hot summer day. While this recipe calls for blending the sour cream into the borscht, some folks like to just plop a dollop on top.

> 1 jar (33 oz.) prepared beet borscht
> 8 oz. sour cream
> 2 cans (16 oz. each) julienne beets
> 1 cucumber, diced
> 4 green onions, diced

Pour beet borscht into a large bowl and mix in sour cream until the mixture is the color of Pepto-Bismol™ and there are no lumps. Add cans of beets (juice and all), cucumber, and green onions. Mix well to blend and then refrigerate until icy cold. Serves 4 to 6.

Cold Summer Cherry Soup

This is definitely an old-world soup, not too popular by today's standards. Because it's so delicious and easy to make, people need to be reminded how good it really is.

2 pounds fresh cherries, pitted
1½ cups dry red wine
2 cups water
½ cup sugar
½ lemon, thinly sliced
1 cinnamon stick
4 whole cloves
½ cup sour cream (optional)

Place all ingredients in saucepan and bring to a boil. Lower heat, cover, and simmer for about 15 minutes. Remove cloves and chill until ready to serve. Top with a dollop of sour cream, if desired. Serves 6.

Grandma's Easy Schav

In the old days, schav was made by chopping, cleaning, and boiling sorrel (sour grass). These days, schav can be found in jars, making the whole process so much easier.

1 jar (33 oz.) schav
½ pint sour cream
4 green onions, cleaned and sliced
1 pkg. (8 oz.) frozen chopped spinach

Pour schav into large serving bowl. Add sour cream and mix until creamy. Add onions and spinach and mix well. Serve chilled. Serves 4.

Rusty's Buttermilk Soup

This is another one of those cool, refreshing soups for a hot summer day, but should be eaten immediately, otherwise the lettuce will wilt. All ingredients should be nice and crunchy.

1 qt. ice-cold buttermilk
½ head iceberg lettuce, chopped
1 cucumber, peeled and coarsely chopped
6 radishes, cleaned and sliced
4 green onions, cleaned and sliced
Salt and pepper to taste

Combine all ingredients and serve immediately. Makes 4 servings.

If you're in a really big hurry, a packaged salad blend can be used. Try to use the kind that has plenty of vegetables, including radishes.

SALADS

❧

Henry behind his deli counter.

Being health-conscious (I was the only kid in school that had whole-wheat fig bars instead of Fig Newtons™ in my lunchbox), Grandma always managed to stuff fresh vegetables down my throat whenever possible.

When I was little and asked for an in-between-meal snack, I was usually given two options: bread and butter or raw vegetables. Not that there weren't cookies in the house—Grandma always had a little stash of her favorite chocolate-covered marshmallow and graham cracker cookies put aside for when she had a craving—but I didn't care for those and I was up to my ears in the aforementioned whole-wheat fig bars, so carrots and celery it was.

I think I finally got to appreciate Grandma's efforts as I got older and decided that I really did like rabbit food, and got a little bit more creative in its preparation. Now, I'd rather eat a big yummy salad than a big fat hunk of meat any day.

We never had mixed-green salads at mealtime and in many restaurants at that time an intact quarter of a head of iceberg lettuce with a dollop of salad dressing was called salad. In Grandma's way of thinking, tuna, eggs, chicken, and potatoes were the ingredients of a true salad, and the only vegetables she'd add to those were celery and onion. Occasionally, when produce was abundant, she'd whip together a chopped salad at the deli, but that's about as far as the creativity went.

Nowadays, salads come in all shapes and forms. A regular tossed salad has evolved from just lettuce and tomato into a bowlful of garden delights, with fresh ingredients never even thought of in years gone by.

The recipes offered here encompass a variety of vegetarian and nonvegetarian delights, some old-world and some that are just plain out of this world.

Crunchy Radish Salad

Radishes and sour cream go quite well together, and the sour cream takes away some of the bite of a strong radish.

> **2 bunches radishes**
> **1 tbsp. olive oil**
> **2 tbsp. vinegar**
> **1 tsp. chopped fresh chives**
> **Salt and pepper to taste**
> **½ cup sour cream for garnish**

Wash and slice radishes. Mix oil, vinegar, chives, salt, and pepper together and pour over radishes. Let stand in the refrigerator for about 2 hours. Serve with a dollop of sour cream. Serves 4.

Grandpa's Onion Salad

There were always onions galore served at every meal and this salad was a nice change of pace from plain sliced raw onions.

> **½ cup olive oil**
> **3 tbsp. vinegar**
> **Salt to taste**
> **2 onions, thinly sliced**
> **Anchovy fillets for garnish**
> **Sliced black olives for garnish**

Mix together oil, vinegar, and salt. Pour over onion slices and top with a few anchovy fillets and black olives. Refrigerate until ready to serve. Serves 4.

Rusty's Stinky Turnips

This is a version of Middle Eastern pickled turnips, but with a lot more garlic, no vinegar, and no beet juice for coloring. They're good for a snack or on a relish plate. You may reek after eating them, but what's a little offensive odor between friends?

> 2 peeled raw turnips, thinly sliced
> 4 green onions, roughly chopped
> ½ cup salad oil (or enough to cover turnips)
> ½ tsp. garlic powder*

Place turnips and onions in glass jar with tight fitting lid. Add oil and garlic powder to cover. Shake well and store jar (she always kept hers in the fridge) for 2 to 3 days before eating. Makes about 1 pint.

*4 cloves of mashed fresh garlic may be substituted.

Grandma's Pickled Cucumbers and Onions

These are so good and incredibly easy to make. They're good for snacking, as a side dish, and terrific on sandwiches.

> 1 cup water
> 1 cup vinegar
> 4 tbsp. sugar
> Salt to taste
> 4 large cucumbers
> 2 large onions

Bring water, vinegar, sugar, and salt to a boil in a saucepan. Meanwhile, peel and slice cucumber into about ½-inch slices, then slice the onion into thin rings. Place veggies in a large bowl and cover with hot vinegar mixture from saucepan. Cover and refrigerate for at least 3 hours before serving, mixing once or twice to make sure all vegetables are well-marinated. Serves 6.

Mrs. Lorincz's Cucumber Salad

Crispy, sweet, and tart all in the same bite—how delicious is that?

    2 medium (about 1¼ lb. total) cucumbers,
        washed and pared
    2 tsp. salt
    3 tbsp. vinegar
    3 tbsp. water
    ½ tsp. sugar
    ¼ tsp. paprika
    ¼ tsp. pepper
    ½ clove garlic, minced
    ¼ tsp. paprika

Thinly slice cucumbers and place in bowl. Sprinkle salt over cucumber slices. Mix lightly and set cucumbers aside for 1 hour (at room temperature). Meanwhile, mix vinegar, water, sugar, paprika, pepper, and garlic together and set aside.

Squeeze cucumber slices a few at a time (discarding liquid) and place into a bowl. Pour vinegar mixture over cucumbers and toss lightly. Sprinkle with paprika. Chill in refrigerator for 1 to 2 hours before serving. Serves 6 to 8.

Rusty's Beet and Horseradish Salad

My mother loved hot, spicy food and beets, so it's only natural that she combined the two to create this mouthwatering salad.

    3 cups diced beets
    2 tbsp. minced green onion
    3 tbsp. salad oil
    1 tsp. salt
    2 tsp. sugar
    6 tbsp. beet horseradish

Drain beets and place in bowl. Mix onion, oil, salt, sugar, and horseradish in a bowl and blend well. Stir in beets and mix thoroughly. Chill before serving. Serves 4.

Easy Beet and Cucumber Salad

It's been my experience that most men don't like beets, but every man I've ever asked can't seem to explain why. Mention the word beets and they just say, "Yuck!" That's okay in my house because then there's more for me.

1 can sliced pickled beets
1 large cucumber, peeled and sliced
1 small onion, finely chopped
1½ cups sour cream
Salt to taste

Drain beets and place in bowl. Add cucumber and onion. Mix in sour cream and blend well, but be careful not to break up beets. Salt to taste and refrigerate for about 1 hour before serving. Serves 4 to 6.

Chunky Gazpacho Salad

If you threw all the ingredients of this rustic, juicy salad into a blender, you'd have a yummy cold soup, but wouldn't get the satisfaction of the crunch. If you have a more delicate palate, you may want to omit the jalapeño and hot sauce. I'll go out on a limb and say that this is my all-time favorite salad.

2 large cucumbers, peeled and diced
2 large tomatoes, diced
½ onion, julienned
1 small jalapeño, cored, seeded, and finely
   diced (optional)
Juice of 2 limes
¼ cup olive oil
¼ cup vinegar
1 tsp. salt
¼ tsp. oregano
¼ tsp. thyme
¼ tsp. basil
1 tbsp. dill weed
Black pepper to taste
Hot sauce to taste

Place vegetables in large bowl. Add lime juice, oil, and vinegar and mix well. Add seasonings and hot sauce and mix well again. Chill until ready to serve and stir well before serving. Serve with a French or sourdough baguette to sop up all the juice. Serves 4.

Slobod's Chopped Salad

This is one of those salads that uses up all the leftover vegetables in your salad bin. In addition to the vegetables mentioned below, be creative and add other veggies like broccoli, cauliflower, or peas.

1 large cucumber, diced
1 large tomato, diced
2 stalks celery, diced
½ onion, diced
1 large carrot, peeled and diced
2 green onions, washed and sliced
6 radishes, diced
¼ lb. fresh green beans, diced
Your favorite salad dressing

Cut up all vegetables and place in bowl. Toss with your favorite salad dressing and serve. Serves 4 to 6.

Grandma's Farmer Salad

Whenever she wanted a quick lunch, Grandma would throw this together and eat it with a piece of matzo. It is also great as a side salad with a cold supper.

> **1 bunch of radishes, sliced**
> **1 bunch of green onions, sliced**
> **2 cucumbers, peeled and thinly sliced**
> **16 oz. cottage cheese**
> **1 pint sour cream**
> **Salt and pepper to taste**

Place all vegetables into a bowl and mix. Then add cottage cheese and season to taste. Place individual servings on a plate and top with a dollop of sour cream. Serves 4.

Slobod's Deli Potato Salad

No meal in our house could be served without the requisite starch. Grandma made this potato salad all the time. It is great for lunch or dinner.

> **3 large potatoes**
> **2 hard-boiled eggs, chopped**
> **½ small onion, chopped**
> **2 celery stalks, diced**
> **¾ cup mayonnaise**
> **2 tbsp. sweet pickle relish**
> **½ tsp. garlic powder**
> **Salt and pepper to taste**

Boil potatoes until soft but not mushy, then drain. When slightly cooled, peel and cut into chunks. Place in large bowl and add remaining ingredients. Mix thoroughly and carefully (so you don't end up with a mashed potato salad) and refrigerate until ready to serve. Taste and adjust seasonings before serving. Serves 4 to 6.

Slobod's Tangy Four-Bean Salad

This sweet and sour bean salad is just so good it's addictive.

1 can (14 oz.) kidney beans
1 can (14 oz.) yellow wax beans
1 can (14 oz.) green beans
1 can (6 oz.) garbanzo beans
½ cup chopped green pepper
½ large onion, chopped
¾ cup sugar
⅔ cup vinegar
⅓ cup oil
Salt and pepper to taste

Drain juices from canned vegetables and place all vegetables in large mixing bowl. In separate bowl, mix together sugar, vinegar, and oil. Mix well and pour over vegetables. Salt and pepper to taste. Let marinate overnight before serving. Serves 4 to 6.

Richard Simmons' Yentl Lentil Salad

Health and fitness guru Richard Simmons has devoted his life to helping people get fit and stay healthy. Usually, healthy foods have gotten a bad reputation as being bland and not the least bit tasty. In the case of this recipe, however, healthy eating is a blessing, not a curse.

> **2 cups cooked lentils**
> **1½ cups peeled, seeded, chopped tomatoes**
> **1 cup chopped parsley**
> **½ cup diced celery**
> **½ cup chopped green pepper**
> **½ cup chopped red onion**
> **¼ cup chopped mint**
> **¼ cup lemon juice**
> **1 tsp. salt**
> **1 tbsp. olive oil**
> **¼ tsp. pepper**
> **⅛ tsp. garlic powder**
> **⅛ tsp. cumin**
> **Lettuce leaves**
> **Mint leaves (optional)**

In large mixing bowl, combine all ingredients except lettuce and mint leaves, mixing thoroughly. Chill. Serve on bed of lettuce. Garnish with mint leaves, if desired. Makes 3 servings.

Slobod's Deli Coleslaw

Grandma liked her coleslaw creamy, with just a hint of sourness. In the deli, they'd often use coleslaw in sandwiches, as well as a side dish.

½ medium cabbage, shredded
1 small carrot, shredded
¼ cup chopped onion
¼ cup mayonnaise
½ cup sour cream
1 tbsp. sugar
2 tsp. lemon or lime juice
½ tsp. celery seed
Salt and pepper to taste

Place cabbage, carrot, and onion in mixing bowl. In separate bowl, blend together mayonnaise, sour cream, sugar, lemon or lime juice, and celery seed. Season with salt and pepper. Pour over vegetables and mix thoroughly. Refrigerate at least 1 hour before serving. Serves 6 to 8.

Slobod's Canned Salmon Salad

Sometimes Grandma would serve this salad as is, but when she wanted a quick hot supper, she'd add a raw egg, form it into patties, coat with bread-crumbs and make fish cakes.

1 can (12 oz.) salmon
2 stalks celery, finely chopped
4 tbsp. mayonnaise
¼ small onion, chopped
2 tbsp. sweet pickle relish
Salt and pepper to taste

Mix all ingredients together and refrigerate until ready to serve. Serves 2 to 4.

Slobod's Tuna Salad

Nothing is simpler than tuna salad. In this version, it's the addition of rosemary that really makes all the flavors pop.

> **1 can (12 oz.) tuna in spring water**
> **¼ cup mayonnaise**
> **1 stalk celery, chopped**
> **¼ cup chopped onion**
> **2 tbsp. sweet pickle relish**
> **¼ tsp. dried rosemary or ½ tsp. fresh**

Place all ingredients into mixing bowl and blend thoroughly. Chill until ready to serve. Serves 2.

Grandma's Tuna Pasta Salad

When Grandma came up with a plain tuna salad recipe she liked, she decided to make it even better by adding a little macaroni.

> **8 oz. small elbow macaroni, cooked**
> **1 can (12 oz.) chunk tuna in spring water**
> **¼ cup chopped onion**
> **¼ cup chopped celery**
> **2 tbsp. sweet pickle relish**
> **½ to ¾ cup mayonnaise**
> **Salt and pepper to taste**

Cook macaroni according to package directions. Drain and set aside.

Mix tuna with onion, celery, pickle relish, mayonnaise, and seasonings. Add cooked macaroni and mix well. If the salad seems a bit dry, stir in a bit more mayonnaise, but it's not supposed to be swimming in dressing. Chill before serving. Serves 2.

Grandpa's Sardine Salad

Some people don't take the time to debone sardines because they don't mind the crunch. I buy the skinless and boneless variety.

> **2 cans (8 oz. each) skinless and boneless**
> **sardines**
> **2 hard-boiled eggs, chopped**
> **1 cup cooked small elbow macaroni**
> **½ cup chopped onion**
> **⅓ cup mayonnaise**
> **Lettuce or cabbage cups**

Chop up sardines and mix carefully but thoroughly with other ingredients so as to not make mush. When ready to serve, spoon into lettuce leaf or small cabbage cups. Serves 4.

Leftover Tongue Salad

As I've mentioned before, tongue doesn't top my list of favorite foods, but I'll eat it in a pinch—if it's doctored up. With this particular salad, my grandmother served it to me as a child and told me it was roast beef. Ah, the innocence of youth.

> **½ cup Miracle Whip™ salad dressing**
> **1 tbsp. hot mustard**
> **2 kosher dill pickles, diced**
> **2 tbsp. white vinegar**
> **¼ tsp. dried dill**
> **Salt and pepper to taste**
> **2 cups leftover tongue, chopped**
> **2 cups boiled potatoes, peeled and diced**

Mix together Miracle Whip™, mustard, pickles, vinegar, dill, salt, and pepper, then combine with tongue and potatoes. Mix well and chill before serving. Serves 2 to 4.

Quick Egg Salad

It's my grandmother's tried-and-true mayonnaise and sweet pickle relish combination that makes this salad so good. As with most recipes, feel free to vary the amount of mayonnaise and pickle relish as you see fit.

> **6 hard-boiled eggs**
> **½ cup mayonnaise**
> **2 tbsp. sweet pickle relish**
> **¼ small onion, finely chopped**
> **Salt and pepper to taste**

Peel and roughly chop the eggs. Mix in mayonnaise, pickle relish, chopped onion, salt, and pepper and blend until creamy. Serves 4.

Aldean's Carrot and Raisin Salad

When I first tasted this delicious salad, I thought Aldean must have spent hours preparing the dressing. When she finally gave me the recipe, I couldn't believe that something so good was so easy to make.

> **3 large carrots, shredded (about 2½ cups)**
> **½ cup raisins**
> **½ cup Miracle Whip™ salad dressing***

Shred carrots and place in mixing bowl. Add raisins and toss well with Miracle Whip™. Chill before serving. Serves 4.

*This recipe does not work well with regular mayonnaise. If you can't use Miracle Whip™, don't make it.

Dressed Fruit Salad

This is one of those fruit salad recipes where you can use any fruit you happen to have on hand. In the summer, use summer fruit, and in the winter, apples, pears, and grapes work just as well. Just mix and match because no matter what fruit you put into it, the dressing makes it taste delicious. A friend of mine says she'd be happy without the fruit and just have the dressing served in a tall glass with a straw.

> 2 large apples, diced
> 1 large banana, sliced
> 3 kiwis, peeled and sliced
> 1 can (6 oz.) chunk pineapple, thoroughly
>   drained
> 1 large ripe pear, diced
> 1 cup seedless grapes

Place all fruit in large serving bowl, cover, and refrigerate.

DRESSING

> 1 container (16 oz.) sour cream
> ½ cup firmly packed brown sugar
> ½ tsp. vanilla extract
> ¼ to ½ tsp. cinnamon

In a bowl, mix together all ingredients (depending on your taste, you might want to vary the amounts of sugar, vanilla, and cinnamon). Mix well. Refrigerate for about 30 minutes to allow flavors to meld.

When serving, place fruit in individual bowls and top with generous dollop of dressing. Serves 6.

Dr. Ruth Westheimer's Sexy Fruit Salad

It was a bite of an apple that started the whole thing. Famed sex therapist Dr. Ruth Westheimer takes that devilish apple to new heights by combining it into this winning fruit salad.

> **2 oranges**
> **2 grapefruits**
> **1 apple**
> **2 pears**
> **2 bananas**
> **2 persimmons, if available**
> **2 kiwis, if available**
> **5 dates**
> **1 cup sliced strawberries**
> **½ cup chopped or shredded coconut**
> **2 tbsp. raisins**
> **2 tbsp. frozen orange juice concentrate**
> **2 tbsp. frozen apple juice concentrate**
> **⅓ cup curaçao or fruit liqueur**
> **¼ cup sweet red wine**
> **Chopped almonds or walnuts (according to taste)**

Section oranges and grapefruits and discard membranes. Place in large bowl. Drain excess juice. Cut up remaining fruit and mix with coconut, raisins, juice concentrates, liqueur, and wine. Refrigerate overnight.

Place in individual fruit bowls, or glasses, and sprinkle with almonds or walnuts. Can also be served in a large bowl as part of your buffet. Optional: If you want to go all out, top each serving with ice cream or whipped cream, or dress with a combination of 1 cup sour cream and 3 tablespoons maple syrup. Serves 4 to 6.

Rusty's Jewish-Italian Salad Dressing

This was my mother's classic house dressing.

1 cup salad oil
½ tsp. grated parmesan cheese
½ tsp. cayenne pepper
½ tsp. black pepper
1 tsp. garlic powder
¼ cup wine vinegar
(Any other spices you like are optional)

Shake all ingredients together in a glass jar and let sit for a day or two before serving. Shake well before using. Yields about 10 ounces.

Rusty's Quick Bleu Cheese Dressing

It's quick and easy, and you can adjust the amount of bleu cheese to your liking. You can also use Roquefort if you prefer.

3 oz. bleu cheese or Roquefort cheese
1 pint sour cream

Crumble cheese into a bowl. Add sour cream and mix thoroughly. Allow to sit at least 2 hours before serving. Yields 1 pint.

SANDWICHES

My stepfather, William McKilligan, enjoying a deli sandwich.

A slice of meat between two slices of bread with a little mustard or mayonnaise slapped on it wasn't the type of sandwich I grew up on. In the first place, we NEVER had white bread in the house—Grandma didn't think it was healthy enough. And processed lunchmeat wasn't high on her list of items to make sandwiches with, either. We had salami aplenty and liverwurst on occasion for cold sandwiches, but we mostly made hot sandwiches out of leftover meat from the night before. I think I must've been in my teens before I ever tasted a bologna sandwich and, with apologies to Oscar Mayer®, I don't think I've had one since. I used to feel like a traitor, because the Oscar Mayer® Wienermobile™ would regularly stop off at the grocery store where my grandfather worked. He and the Oscar of the day got to know each other very well and Grandpa would bring home dozens of little "weenie whistles" for me to play with. And I still hated bologna.

I recently heard the results of a food survey saying that most American children will eat, on average, about fifteen hundred peanut butter and jelly sandwiches before they graduate high school. That was another sandwich I only had at friends' houses. Grandma did buy peanut butter, but it was the natural kind that separated in the jar and didn't look very appetizing, even after you stuck in a knife and tried to mix it up. I didn't feel too deprived, though, because big and tasty deli sandwiches were always on the menu at our house. Being a butcher in his later years, Grandpa always brought home the best cuts of meat and poultry to make the same kind of yummy sandwiches they made back in Philadelphia.

A lot of people think hearty deli sandwiches are hard to make but, in truth, once you have the right ingredients, they are pretty easy to slap together and well worth the effort. This chapter includes some of Slobod's Deli's best.

Slobod's Fried Salami and Egg Sandwich

We all grew up on fried egg sandwiches, so why not embellish on a classic? This omelet sandwich is also good made with a bagel or English muffin.

2 eggs
Butter for frying
3 oz. salami, cubed
1 tsp. catsup, mustard, or mayonnaise
2 slices toasted egg bread
Slice of raw onion

Beat eggs in bowl. Melt butter in frying pan and add eggs and salami. Scramble together until done to your liking. Spread favorite condiment on bread and transfer scrambled eggs and salami to bread. Top with slice of onion. Makes 1 sandwich.

Deli Beef BLT

Beef bacon is a nice change even for those who do eat pork. It may not be as easy to find as regular bacon, but certainly worth the search. Of course, you can use any kind of bacon you like.

1 lb. beef bacon
8 bagels, sliced in half and toasted
Mayonnaise to taste
Sliced tomato
Lettuce leaves

Fry bacon until crispy, then place on paper towels and pat off grease. Set aside. Toast bagels and then spread each slice with mayonnaise. Add lettuce, tomatoes, and bacon. Makes 8 sandwiches.

Corned Beef or Pastrami on Rye

On Friday nights, customers of Slobod's Deli would line up around the block and wait for Grandpa to put out the "Fresh Corned Beef" sign, because once that was up, a thick juicy sandwich wasn't far behind. Making this sandwich is a no-brainer. There are no specific amounts of meat given because it's up to you how high you want to pile this classic sandwich. Non-Jews have been known to eat corned beef sandwiches with lettuce, tomato, and mayonnaise on white bread. They just don't know any better.

> **Mustard**
> **Corned beef or pastrami, thinly sliced**
> **2 slices Jewish or corn rye bread**

Spread mustard on bread and pile on the meat. Serve with a big, fat dill pickle and a little cole slaw or potato salad on the side. Makes 1 sandwich.

Slobod's Deli Reuben

There's something about the tangy sauerkraut in this toasted treat that makes your mouth water even before you take your first bite. At the deli, they piled this sandwich a mile high. You may not want to insult your cholesterol to that extreme, so please feel free to vary amounts to your liking. Just don't use anything other than rye bread—that would be a mortal sin.

> **1 tbsp. butter or margarine for frying**
> **2 slices rye bread**
> **1 tbsp. Thousand Island dressing**
> **1 slice Swiss cheese**
> **¼ lb. corned beef or pastrami, thinly sliced**
> **4 oz. sauerkraut, drained**

Heat a frying pan or griddle over medium heat. While pan is heating, butter one side of each slice of bread. With buttered side face down, liberally spread dressing over one slice. Then put slice of cheese, meat, and sauerkraut on top. Place other slice of bread buttered side up on top. Carefully transfer to warmed skillet and cook until lightly browned on the bottom. Then gently flip the sandwich over and cook until the other side is lightly browned and cheese is melted. Makes 1 sandwich.

Avocado Jack Burger

This is a glorified cheeseburger with an avocado bonus. If possible, it's best to use Hass avocados because of their exceptionally creamy texture. If you like your sandwiches spicy, try a jalapeño jack cheese.

¼ lb. ground beef
1 hamburger bun, toasted
½ ripe avocado, sliced
1 slice jack cheese
Salt and pepper to taste

Form meat into patty and cook to desired doneness. Place cooked meat on one half of toasted bun. Top with avocado and then cheese. Season to taste. Place under the broiler just until cheese melts. Top with remaining half of bun. Makes 1 burger.

Smothered Onion and Mushroom Burger

Is there a better combination than mushrooms and onions? Not unless you top a burger with some. There is no need to use condiments like mayonnaise on this sandwich because the olive oil that the mushrooms and onions are sautéed in helps keep this burger juicy.

    ¼ lb. ground beef
    1 small onion, sliced
    5 or 6 fresh mushrooms, sliced
    2 tbsp. olive oil
    ⅛ tsp. garlic powder
    Salt and pepper to taste
    1 kaiser roll

Shape the ground beef into a patty and fry to desired doneness. In a separate pan, while meat is frying, sauté onion and mushrooms in olive oil until caramelized. Season with garlic powder, salt, and pepper.

To build burger, place meat on one half of Kaiser roll. Top with onion and mushroom mixture. Cover with remaining half of roll. Makes 1 burger.

Deli Bleu Cheese Burger

You're right—mixing cheese and meat isn't kosher. But, oy, what a delicious combination. You can atone for the sin of eating this on Yom Kippur. Meanwhile, enjoy!

    ¼ lb. ground beef
    2 tbsp. bleu cheese dressing
    1 hamburger bun, toasted
    1 lettuce leaf
    1 tomato slice
    Salt and pepper to taste

Shape the ground beef into a patty and sauté until desired doneness. Build the burger by putting 1 tbsp. bleu cheese dressing on one half of toasted bun (you can add more or less dressing according to your taste). Add burger, lettuce, and tomato. Season to taste. Spread remaining dressing on other half of the bun and top the burger. This is one of those burgers that will require several napkins. Makes 1 burger.

Slobod's Patty Melt

Simply speaking, a patty melt is a hamburger minus the bun, lettuce, and tomato. It's traditionally grilled on rye bread and loaded with savory sautéed onions. If you're not a fan of rye, you could use sourdough, pumpernickel, or any other bread with a dense consistency.

    2 slices rye bread
    1 tsp. butter
    ½ small onion, sliced
    1 tsp. oil
    ¼ lb. ground beef
    1 slice cheddar cheese

Spread each slice of bread with butter. Set aside. In a frying pan, sauté onion in oil until golden brown and caramelized. Remove from pan and set aside. Shape ground beef patty to fit bread and then fry in the same pan used for the onions. When fried to desired doneness, place ground beef on dry side of bread, top with cheese slice, and then top with grilled onions. Place other slice of bread on top, buttered side up. Transfer to warmed frying pan or griddle and fry until golden brown. Turn and fry other side until golden brown and cheese has melted. Makes 1 sandwich.

Oh-So-Good Brisket Sandwich

The combination of melted cheese on warm brisket makes this a truly mouthwatering offering, especially with a big, fat dill pickle on the side.

    2 slices rye bread
    Mayonnaise to taste
    ¼ lb. thinly sliced brisket
    1 slice swiss cheese

Spread one slice of bread with mayonnaise. Top with brisket, swiss cheese, and remaining slice of bread. Pop into microwave for about a minute—just long enough to allow the cheese to melt. Serve immediately. Makes 1 sandwich.

Grab-Your-Napkin Turkey Sandwich

This is one of the all-time great cold turkey sandwiches and should be made with real, not processed, turkey.

> **2 slices rye bread**
> **1 tsp. Thousand Island dressing**
> **¼ lb. sliced turkey**
> **1 slice swiss cheese**
> **2 slices tomato**
> **1 slice raw onion**
> **Lettuce to your liking**

Spread bread with dressing, pile on the turkey, and add remaining ingredients. Makes 1 sandwich.

Crunchy Turkey Sandwich

Why would someone sabotage a perfectly healthy turkey sandwich by adding potato chips? Because it tastes good!

> **2 tbsp. Thousand Island dressing**
> **2 slices of your favorite bread**
> **3 oz. sliced turkey**
> **1 big slice tomato**
> **1 lettuce leaf**
> **A handful of your favorite potato chips**

Spread one tablespoon of Thousand Island dressing on each slice of bread. Add remaining ingredients on top, placing potato chips last. Cover with the other slice of bread and squash the sandwich with your hands to break up the chips, making it easier to pick up and eat. Makes 1 messy sandwich.

Slobod's Not-So-Kosher Club Sandwich

In a proper kosher home, meat and dairy should never be served together, but in a classic club sandwich, you can't *not* mix them. The only concession made here is that beef bacon is used, but feel free to substitute any kind of bacon that suits you.

> **12 slices toasted bread**
> **Mayonnaise to taste**
> **12 slices beef bacon**
> **2 medium tomatoes, thinly sliced**
> **Lettuce leaves**
> **¾ lb. sliced white meat turkey**
> **12 slices Swiss or jack cheese**

For each sandwich, spread a slice of toast with mayonnaise. Top with 2 slices of bacon, 3 tomato slices, and a leaf of lettuce. Top with another slice of toast. Place a little turkey, 1 slice of cheese, and another lettuce leaf on that slice. Top with a third slice of toast, mayonnaise side down. Secure with toothpicks and cut each sandwich into 4 triangles. Makes 4 sandwiches.

Thanksgiving on a Roll

In my opinion, you shouldn't get to eat turkey and cranberry sauce together only once a year. This recipe saves you the trouble of roasting the bird, but still gives you that warm, fuzzy feeling of the holidays.

> **¼ lb. ground turkey**
> **1 hoagie roll, toasted or grilled**
> **2 tbsp. cranberry sauce**

Form the ground turkey into an oblong patty and fry until well done. Place turkey on one half of the toasted roll. Top with cranberry sauce. Makes 1 sandwich.

Jewish Hero

This sandwich tastes exceptionally good with turkey although you can use just about any variety (and any amount) of sliced meat that pleases you.

> **1 large, long sourdough baguette**
> **Mayonnaise to taste**
> **2 sliced tomatoes**
> **Several lettuce leaves**
> **1 onion, thinly sliced**
> **6 slices cheddar cheese**
> **6 slices jack cheese**
> **½ lb. sliced turkey**
> **¼ tsp. oregano**
> **1 tsp. vinegar**
> **1 tsp. olive oil**
> **Sliced olives to taste**
> **Salt and pepper to taste**

Cut baguette in half and slather both sides with mayonnaise. On one half, layer tomatoes, lettuce, onion, cheeses, and turkey. Top with oregano, vinegar, oil, olives, salt, and pepper. Top with remaining half of baguette and cut into quarters. Secure with a toothpick and serve immediately. Makes about 4 individual sandwiches.

Ginny's Hot Chicken Breast Sandwich

Each sandwich is a meal in itself. There are only a few specific amounts given because this is one of those "build-your-own" types of sandwiches where you can vary ingredients to your liking. And trust me—you will like it.

8 whole skinless, boneless chicken breasts
Garlic powder to taste
Oregano to taste
Salt and pepper to taste
½ cup fresh lemon juice
8 hoagie buns, sliced
Mayonnaise to taste
Lettuce leaves
Sliced tomatoes
Sliced raw onions
Sliced avocados

Place chicken breasts over medium heat in dry frying pan. Sprinkle breasts with seasonings to coat and fry in lemon juice until golden brown on each side, but still juicy. You'll need to add the lemon juice in drips here and there to avoid pan from drying out—don't pour it all in at once. When the chicken is done, place buns in oven long enough just to heat through, then spread with mayonnaise, and pile on the chicken, lettuce, tomatoes, onions, and avocados. Makes 8 sandwiches.

Liverwurst to Die For

People either love liverwurst or hate it. If you're not a fan of this tasty lunch meat, just go ahead and skip to the next recipe. If you're still with me, give this delicious sandwich a try. You can use any sort of bread you want, but there's just something about using dill rye that gives this sandwich that extra zing.

> 2 slices dill rye bread
> 1 tsp. mayonnaise
> 1 tsp. sweet pickle relish
> 2 slices liverwurst
> 1 slice raw onion

Spread bread with mayonnaise and relish. Top with liverwurst and onion. Makes 1 sandwich.

Mom's Tuna and Egg Salad Sandwich

While some people are purists and have to have either a tuna or an egg salad sandwich, those who like to be a little more adventurous will love this combination. The tuna spices up the egg and the egg cuts the fishy tuna taste.

> 1 can (6 oz.) tuna
> 2 hard-boiled eggs, chopped
> 1 stalk celery, diced
> 1 slice raw onion, diced
> 2 tbsp. mayonnaise
> 1 tsp. sweet pickle relish
> Salt and pepper to taste
> 4 slices of your favorite bread

Place tuna and chopped eggs in mixing bowl. Add celery, onion, mayonnaise, and relish. Mix well and season to taste. Spread mixture on bread. Makes 2 sandwiches.

Rusty's Favorite Anchovy Sandwich

This is not a sandwich for the faint of heart or those on a sodium-restricted diet. You don't need to use any sort of condiment on this sandwich because of the anchovy oil.

> 4 flat anchovy fillets
> 2 slices of your favorite bread
> 4 cucumber slices, sliced paper thin
> 1 slice raw onion, sliced paper thin

Build your sandwich by placing the 4 anchovy fillets on a slice of bread in a single layer. Top with cucumber, onion, and remaining slice of bread. Makes 1 sandwich.

Grandma's Mashed Avocado Sandwich

Grandma had a bit of Johnny Appleseed in her. One day she took an avocado pit and just stuck it in the ground. Five years later, the tree was up over the rooftop and its roots had pushed up half the driveway—good thing she didn't own a car! It was quite a prolific bloomer, so after she had given avocados away to everyone who'd take them, she had to figure out a quick and easy way to use them up in her own kitchen and that gave birth to her famous mashed avocado sandwich.

> 1 ripe avocado
> 2 slices bread, toasted
> Salt and pepper to taste

Mash avocado in a bowl. Add salt and pepper and spread on toast. Serves 1.

ENTRÉES

When Grandpa came back from a fishing trip,
Grandma made her Sweet and Sour Fish.

To Grandma, entrées were the meal. Everything that was served before or after the entrée was insignificant. After stuffing up on appetizers, soup, and salad, one might think there would be very little room for a meat-and-pota-toes-type main course, but who are you kidding? When those delicious odors wafted in from the kitchen, there was no question about politely declining or getting around it by taking smaller portions. Remember, it was my grand-mother's mission in life to feed people, and feed them well. The minute every-one was seated, she would start passing the plates so fast it would make your head spin. The words "diet," "moderation," or "no thank you" were not in her vocabulary.

Aldean's husband, Jack, was Grandma's ideal dinner guest. He would walk into the house with only one thing on his mind: food. If the idle chitchat of hellos took too long, he'd interrupt the conversation by asking, "Do you all believe in the hereafter?" Then he'd walk toward the dining room table, already laden with appetizers, pull out his chair, sit down, and proclaim, "Well, this is what I'm here after!" So much for small talk.

Relatives told me they wouldn't eat all day and would wear their loosest fit-ting clothes when they knew they'd be having dinner at our house. Halfway through the meal, the men would have to loosen their belts a notch and, after dinner, would waddle into the living room and plop down on the nearest couch or armchair. The women would all gather in the kitchen to wash and dry the dishes, and it wouldn't be long before we could hear a chorus of snores coming from the living room. Those snores were music to Grandma's ears because they were proof of full bellies.

Bernie Kopell's Roast Turkey

Actor Ray Milland shared this recipe with Bernie during one of their *Love Boat* voyages together, and now Bernie prepares it every holiday season to rave reviews. According to Milland, "It is the absolutely only sensible way to cook the bird." Bernie wholeheartedly agrees.

> **One turkey**
> **Extra virgin olive oil**
> **Spike® seasoning to taste**
> **Onion powder to taste**
> **Garlic powder to taste**
> **Cut-up onions, chopped celery, and fresh**
>   **garlic cloves to taste, but enough to fill**
>   **the cavity of the bird**
> **1 cup of sherry (not cooking sherry)**
> **4 or 5 medium onions, cut in half**

Here's how Bernie says to put it all together:

"Remove the giblets from the bird and rinse thoroughly. Get the best extra virgin olive oil you can find and rub it all over the turkey, inside and out. If you can find that marvelous Gaylord [Hauser] seasoning, Spike®, use it in the cavity and on the outside of the bird along with the onion and garlic powder. What you want to stuff the bird with is as much cut-up onions, celery, and fresh garlic (to taste) as it will hold. After you've done all that, pour a cup of sherry into the cavity and sew it up. And here's the trick: Do this the night before you cook it, allowing the flavors to absorb into the bird. Cover and put into the fridge. The next morning, set your oven to 325 degrees and start baking your bird with the breast up for the first half of the baking time. Then— and this is the most important part—flip the turkey breast over for the remainder of the cooking time, and secure some onion halves, flat side down, with steel cooking pins, along the back of the turkey. Of course, you want to keep it covered. For the hour and half of baking, baste regularly, allowing those marvelous juices to saturate the breast. Do that, my friend, and you'll have the tenderest, moistest, most succulent turkey that's guaranteed to bring tears to your eyes. Wolfgang Puck, eat your heart out!"

Not-Just-For-Thanksgiving Baked Turkey Breast

What a great, simple meal. It fills the house with the scent of Thanksgiving every time you prepare it, and makes great turkey sandwiches for lunch the next day.

> 1 whole turkey breast
> 1 tsp. oil
> 1 tsp. poultry seasoning
> ½ tsp. garlic powder
> ¼ tsp. onion powder
> ¼ tsp. thyme
> ¼ tsp. oregano
> Salt and pepper to taste

Coat the breast with oil. Sprinkle on seasonings and bake at 325 degrees until golden brown and a meat thermometer reads 190 degrees and the juices run clear. For a 1- to 2-pound breast, this should be after about an hour; for a 3- to 5-pound breast, check after an hour and a half. Baste occasionally.

If the turkey is getting too well done on the outside, lightly drape it with a sheet of aluminum foil for the remaining cooking time. Serves 4 to 6.

Slobod's Baked Chicken

Contrary to lots of other Jewish grandmothers, my Grandma didn't usually roast chicken, she baked it. When you see how easy this dish is to prepare, you'll never roast again.

> 1 roasting chicken (about 3 lb.), cut up
>   into serving-sized pieces
> 1 tsp. oregano
> 1 tsp. poultry seasoning
> ½ tsp. garlic powder
> ½ tsp. onion powder
> Salt and pepper to taste

Place chicken in a roasting dish. Season and bake at 350 degrees for about an hour and fifteen minutes until brown. Serves 4.

Smothered Chicken

Smothered chicken is similar to chicken cacciatore. The slow baking gives all the ingredients a chance to blend well and, when it's done, the chicken will be falling off the bone and will melt in your mouth.

> 1 fresh (not frozen) chicken, cut up into
>   serving-sized pieces
> 1 large carrot, sliced
> 1 large potato, cut into cubes
> 1 tsp. garlic powder
> ¼ tsp. basil
> ½ tsp. thyme
> ¼ tsp. oregano
> Salt and pepper to taste
> 1 large onion, sliced into rings
> 1 can (16 oz.) diced tomatoes

Place the chicken in a large casserole dish. Surround with sliced carrot and potato cubes. Sprinkle with spices, top with onion rings. Pour canned tomatoes over chicken. Cover tightly with foil and bake in a 350 degree oven for about 2 hours. When chicken is swimming in liquid and falling off the bone, it's done. Serves 4.

Carrie's Peachy Chicken

This invention of Carrie's is a sweet and easy way to prepare chicken. Just schmear on the preserves and pop it in the oven.

> 1 jar (16 oz.) favorite peach preserves
> 1 skinlessroasting chicken, cut up into
>   serving-sized pieces
> 1 jar (16 oz.) orange marmalade

Spread the peach preserves on the bottom of an aluminum pan. Place chicken pieces on top of preserves. Cover chicken with orange marmalade. Bake uncovered at 350 degrees for about 1½ hours. Serves 4.

Grandma's Sweet Stuffed Chicken

This chicken dish is so sweet and yummy, it could easily pass for a dessert.

½ lb. pitted prunes
¼ lb. dried apricots, diced
¼ lb. apples, diced
4-lb. roasting chicken
Salt and pepper to taste

Soak prunes and apricots in water for about 30 minutes. While they're soaking, dice the apple and wash the chicken. Pat the chicken dry and sprinkle the cavity with salt. Drain the dried fruit, but reserve the liquid. Season the chicken with salt and pepper, and then loosely fill the cavity with the fruit. Roast in a 350-degree oven for about 45 minutes, basting regularly with pan drippings and the reserved fruit liquid.

When chicken is done, remove to a platter. Wait a few minutes before carving. You can also cut the chicken into fourths and serve stuffing on the side. Serves 4.

Aldean's Liver Kugel

Kugels come in all varieties, from rice to noodle to potato. While this liver kugel isn't as popular as some of the others, it is a nice, delicious change of pace for an evening meal.

½ lb. egg noodles, cooked
1 onion, diced
1 lb. chicken livers, cooked
2 tbsp. schmaltz
3 eggs
½ cup melted schmaltz
Salt and pepper to taste

Cook noodles according to package directions.
Sauté onion and liver in a frying pan in 2 tablespoons schmaltz until onions are caramelized and liver is thoroughly cooked. Remove from pan and cut liver into small pieces.

Beat eggs in large bowl, then add noodles, liver, onions, the melted schmaltz, salt, and pepper. Blend well and place in a greased 2-quart casserole. Bake at 375 degrees until top is lightly browned. Serves 4.

Grandma's Fried Chicken Livers and Onions

Even folks who say they can't stand liver might have a change of heart when the intoxicating aroma of liver and onions fills the house.

1 lb. chicken livers
1 to 2 tsp. vegetable cooking oil
2 large onions, sliced
2 cloves of garlic, diced
Salt and pepper to taste

Prepare the liver by rinsing well and removing the yellow bits that are attached. They are edible, but add a bitter taste. Set aside after cleaning and rinsing.

Heat a large skillet over medium heat. Place oil in pan and add onions. Sauté until onions begin to get translucent, then add garlic and livers. Fry until livers are thoroughly cooked and onions are caramelized. Salt and pepper to taste. Serves 2.

Pupik Fricassee

Fricassee is a French term for meat, especially chicken or veal, browned lightly, stewed, and served in a sauce made with its own stock. Pupik means "bellybutton" in Yiddish, but in this recipe the term refers to all giblets.

> 1 cup diced onions
> 4 tbsp. Nyafat™ or vegetable oil
> 2 lb. mixed giblets
> 2 cloves garlic, diced
> Salt and pepper to taste
> 2 tbsp. flour
> 4 cups boiling water

In a saucepan, brown onions in fat, then add giblets, garlic, salt, and pepper, and brown. Sprinkle with flour, add the boiling water, cover, and cook over low heat for about an hour, or until tender. Serves 4.

Rusty's Flanken

Some people mistake flanken for short ribs, but they're not the same. Years ago, flanken was considered scrap meat—a lesser cut you could buy cheaply. Lately, flanken is much more popular and has soared in price. Depending on where you live, flanken might be difficult, but not impossible, to find.

> Nonstick cooking spray
> 2 lb. flanken
> ½ tsp. garlic powder
> Salt and pepper to taste

Heat oven to 350 degrees. Spray a roasting pan with nonstick cooking spray. There is enough fat on the flanken that you won't need to butter the pan. (I cover the pan with heavy duty foil for easier cleanup.) Place the flanken in pan, season, and bake for at least an hour, or a little longer if it still shows pink. Cool and drain on paper towels. Then enjoy. Serves 2.

Melt-in-Your-Mouth Short Ribs

Yes, short ribs are expensive and a bit fatty, but this isn't a dish you'd eat every day. Once in a while, everyone needs to splurge.

3 lb. beef short ribs
¼ cup honey
1 cup beef broth
1 cup catsup
Dash of Worcestershire sauce
Salt and pepper to taste
2 onions, thinly sliced
2 large carrots, sliced

Broil ribs in broiler pan 5 to 10 minutes, or until brown. While ribs are browning, mix honey, beef broth, catsup, and Worcestershire sauce together and set aside. Sauté vegetables until soft and place in a roasting pan. When ribs are done, place on top of vegetables. Pour sauce over ribs. Cover and bake at 350 degrees for about 2 hours, turning ribs once or twice during baking. Serves 4.

Rusty's Wheat Germ Meat Loaf

Some may think wheat germ is a strange ingredient for a meat loaf, but it adds a wonderfully nutty taste . . . and is healthy, too!

1 lb. lean ground beef
1 small onion, diced
½ lb. chopped mushrooms
1 tbsp. roasted wheat germ
1 large egg
Your favorite meat loaf seasonings to taste

Preheat oven to 350 degrees. Mix all ingredients in a large bowl. Transfer mixture to a meat loaf pan. Bake for 1 hour or until top of meat loaf isn't wet. Wait about five minutes before slicing. The nutty flavor from the wheat germ really makes this meat loaf special. Serves 4.

Grandma's Stuffed Cabbage

Grandma would always simmer her stuffed cabbage in the same sweet and sour broth she used to make her hot cabbage borscht. *So* good!

> **2 lb. short ribs**
> **1½ qt. water**
> **1 onion, diced**
> **2 cups canned tomatoes**
> **Juice of 2 lemons**
> **¼ cup brown sugar**
> **2 tsp. salt**
> **Pepper to taste**

Bring meat to a rapid boil in water. Skim off scum; add onion and tomatoes. Bring again to a boil, lower heat, and simmer for about 2 hours.

Add lemon juice, brown sugar, salt, and pepper. Simmer about 10 minutes more, taste, and adjust seasonings.

The amounts of lemon juice and brown sugar in this sweet and sour soup will vary according to taste. Some prefer it sweeter and others like it more on the tart side. Start with the amounts listed above and then add more of one or the other to suit your taste. Remove short ribs before adding stuffed cabbage leaves; the ribs will make a delicious meal on their own with a couple of boiled potatoes on the side.

STUFFED CABBAGE LEAVES

> **1 large head of cabbage, cored**
> **4 qt. salted water for boiling cabbage**
> ** leaves**
> **1½ lb. ground beef**
> **½ small onion, minced**
> **1 egg**
> **Salt and pepper to taste**

Trim and separate cabbage leaves from cored cabbage and cook in salted boiling water for about 5 minutes. Drain. While leaves are cooking, mix together meat, onion, egg, salt, and pepper. Place 2 tablespoons of filling into each cabbage leaf, and roll up as you would a blintz, making sure the ends are tucked in. Carefully place stuffed leaves in a large dutch oven in layers. Cover with borscht broth and simmer over low heat for about 45 minutes to an hour. Serves 6 to 8.

Gertrud's Rouladen

This recipe comes from a friend whose mother was a really terrific cook. Even though this is a labor-intensive recipe, it's well worth the time spent making it.

> 3 to 4 lb. top round, cut into 10 very thin
>   slices and pounded into rectangular
>   shapes, about 3 to 5 inches
> 10 tsp. mustard
> 2 cups finely chopped onion
> 2 cups finely chopped raw bacon
> Salt and pepper to taste
> 3 tbsp. butter

Lay out beef rectangles on the counter. Evenly spread 1 teaspoon of mustard on each piece of meat, then spread equal amounts of onion and bacon in a thin layer on top of each slice of meat. Salt and pepper to taste. Tightly roll each piece of stuffed meat into a fat cigar shape and secure with a toothpick. Brown meat on all sides in butter over medium heat in a frying pan. When meat is brown, transfer (along with pan drippings) to casserole dish and bake at 350 degrees for about 40 minutes. After cooking, remove meat from dish and set aside. Place pan drippings in a frying pan, and proceed to make the gravy.

GRAVY

> 16 oz. sour cream
> ¾ cup buttermilk
> 1 beef bouillon cube
> ¼ cup flour
> ⅛ cup cornstarch

Add sour cream, buttermilk, bouillon cube, flour, and cornstarch to pan drippings. Mix well and simmer, stirring frequently, until heated through and thick.

To serve, place meat on serving platter and pour gravy on top. Serve with Gertrud's red cabbage (see following recipe).

Gertrud's Red Cabbage

The perfect accompaniment to rouladen.

> 2 heads of red cabbage, shredded
> ½ cup vinegar
> ½ to ¾ cup sugar
> 1 tbsp. salt
> 1 tsp. black pepper
> 20 whole cloves
> 1 or 2 apples, finely chopped
> 1 onion, finely chopped (optional)
> 1 cup water
> 1 cup lard

Blanch red cabbage in boiling water until soft, but still on the crispy side. Add vinegar and simmer over low heat for 10 to 15 minutes. Add remaining ingredients and simmer for another 15 minutes until cabbage is soft, but not mushy. Stir often. When done, add lard and mix through over low heat. Serve cabbage and rouladen together with boiled potatoes. This is a great make-ahead dish because it tastes even better the second day.

Slobod's Swiss Steak

One pot meals are a blessing. And when they taste with such little effort, you're doubly blessed.

> ¼ cup flour
> ½ tsp. garlic powder
> ¼ tsp. oregano
> Salt and pepper to taste
> 2 lb. round steak
> 3 tbsp. oil
> 1 can (15 oz.) tomatoes
> 1 or 2 sliced onions
> 1 green pepper, seeded, cored, and sliced
>   into rings
> 1 celery stalk, diced

Combine flour with seasonings and dredge serving-size pieces of meat in mixture. Pat to remove excess. Brown meat in oil in a deep skillet, and then add tomatoes, onion, pepper, and celery. Bring to a boil, then reduce heat, cover, and simmer for about an hour, or until meat is tender. Serve with mashed potatoes smothered in the leftover gravy. Serves 4 to 6.

Deli Brisket

Some people bake brisket, others boil it. At Slobod's Deli, the brisket was always boiled until tender and juicy, and then sliced thin for sandwiches or thicker for a main course. Remember, always let your brisket cool down before slicing, and make sure you slice against the grain. Otherwise it will be leathery and tough. The same goes for corned beef.

3 lb. beef brisket
1 bay leaf
1 medium onion, quartered
1 medium carrot, sliced
3 cloves garlic
Pinch of oregano
1 bay leaf
2 tsp. salt

Place brisket in large Dutch oven and cover with water. Add rest of the ingredients. Bring to a boil, then cover and simmer for about 3 hours or until tender. Remove from heat and let meat cool in broth for about 15 minutes before serving. Serves 8.

Betty's Mock Chinese Dinner

Betty says this recipe has been in her family for generations. Because she cannot eat sugar, she substitutes artificial sweetener with excellent results.

> **1 lb. ground chuck**
> **¼ cup soy sauce (low sodium, if desired)**
> **¾ cup water**
> **2 cups chopped broccoli**
> **1 tbsp. sugar, or 1 pkg. artificial sweetener**
> **1 small can water chestnuts (optional)**
> **Bean sprouts (optional)**
> **1 cup uncooked white rice**

Cook chuck in frying pan and drain. Mix soy sauce with water and add to meat. Add remaining ingredients, except for rice. Mix well, cover pan, and simmer on low. While beef is cooking, cook rice according to package directions. When rice is done, so is the meat mixture. Serve meat on top of rice. Serves 4 to 6.

Deli Gedempte Fleisch

I always used to call this dish "sweet meat." Grandma used to make it often; it was a tasty way to prepare an economical chuck steak.

> **2 onions, sliced**
> **3 cloves garlic, minced**
> **2 tsp. oil**
> **4 lb. chuck steak**
> **1 stalk celery, diced**
> **2 carrots, diced**
> **1 tsp. salt, or to taste**
> **3 bay leaves**
> **6 peppercorns**
> **8 oz. canned tomatoes**
> **2 tbsp. brown sugar**

In a Dutch oven, brown onions and garlic in oil. Remove onions and garlic from pan and brown meat in leftover drippings. Return onions and garlic to skillet and add remaining ingredients. Bring to a boil and reduce heat, cover, and simmer about 2 hours until meat is tender. While some people like to thicken the gravy with a little cornstarch or flour, Grandma preferred to leave the gravy soupy and serve it over mashed or boiled potatoes. Serves 8 to 10.

Deli Pot Roast with Onions and Carrots

People have been eating pot roast since the invention of the pot. It's comfort food, and so easy to make on a busy day either on top of the stove, in the oven, or in a slow cooker.

> **3 lb. chuck or bottom round roast**
> **2 large onions, quartered**
> **6 carrots, sliced**
> **8 small potatoes, halved**
> **¼ tsp. oregano**
> **¼ tsp. garlic powder**
> **Dash of Worcestershire sauce**
> **1 bay leaf**
> **Salt and pepper to taste**
> **1 can (16 oz.) tomatoes**
> **Water**

Place beef in large baking dish and surround meat with onions, carrots, and potatoes. Sprinkle with seasoning, then add tomatoes. Fill tomato can with water and add to dish. Cover with foil and bake at 350 degrees for about 2 ½ hours or until meat is thoroughly cooked and tender. Serves 6.

Grandpa's Favorite Corned Beef and Cabbage

These days, when you buy a corned beef, the pickling spices are usually included in the packaging. You just plop the beef into water, add the spices, and you're good to go. Grandpa used his own spices and marinated the beef for several days before boiling. One thing to remember when making corned beef is that it must be boiled slowly, about 25 to 30 minutes per pound of beef. Let it come slowly to a boil, and then let it simmer.

4 qt. water
1½ cups salt
1 tbsp. sugar
2 tbsp. pickling spices
½ oz. saltpeter
8 bay leaves
10 cloves garlic
5 lb. corned beef brisket
2 onions
2 stalks celery

First make up the brine. Combine all the spices, including bay leaves and garlic, in the water, bring to a boil and simmer for about 10 minutes. Cool. Then place beef in a nonmetal bowl and pour brine over meat. Weigh meat down with heavy plate or pan to keep it covered in liquid. Let marinate in refrigerator for up to one week.

To cook, rinse off brine, then place meat in a big pot and cover with water. Add onions and celery and cook over low heat according to weight, until tender. Drain, let cool, then slice crosswise, against the grain. Since this dish is usually served with boiled cabbage or potatoes, you can add some to the corned beef pot the last hour of cooking to enhance their flavor. Serves about 12.

Bobby Vinton's Mother's "Gotomki"

The Polish word for this dish is golabki. This delicious stuffed cabbage appeared in my first celebrity cookbook to rave reviews.

2 medium heads of cabbage (cut core so
   leaves will separate when boiled)
1 medium onion, chopped and sautéed till limp
1 can (4 oz.) mushrooms
1 cup cooked white rice
1 lb. mild pork sausage, sautéed
¾ lb. beef, sautéed
1 egg
1 tsp. paprika
½ tsp. marjoram
½ cup skim or low-fat milk
¼ cup warm water
2 tbsp. flour
Salt and pepper to taste
1 can (14 to 16 oz.) tomato sauce

Place cabbage into a large pot. Boil until leaves fall from head. Set leaves aside. Sautée chopped onion with mushrooms. Add onions and mushrooms to cooked rice, pork, and beef. Mix. Add egg, paprika, marjoram, milk, water, flour, salt, and pepper. Fold mixture so ingredients are thoroughly mixed. Spoon and place mixture into the center of one cabbage leaf. Fold one side of the leaf over mixture and remaining side over the folded leaf to enclose mixture and create a cabbage roll. Repeat. Place gotomki in a large tray in single rolls. (To keep rolls from opening, place "seam down.") Cover with aluminum foil and bake at 350 degrees for 2 hours or until gotomki can be cut with a fork. When done, pour tomato sauce over rolls, re-cover with foil and bake at 300 degrees for 45 minutes. Yields about 2 dozen, depending on size of cabbage leaves. Makes about 2 dozen cabbage rolls, depending on the size you make them.

Slobod's Deli Pickled Tongue

My grandparents actually used the same brine for tongue as they did for corned beef, with delicious results.

 1 beef tongue
 1½ cups salt
 1 tbsp. sugar
 2 tbsp. pickling spices
 ½ oz. saltpeter
 8 bay leaves
 10 cloves garlic
 2 onions
 2 stalks celery

Wash meat and then combine all ingredients in a large kettle. Cover with water, bring to a boil, and simmer over medium heat for about 3 hours, or until tender. Let the tongue cool down in the water, and then remove the skin, slice, and serve. Serves 6.

Aldean's Baked Herring

Whether it's served hot or cold, baked herring and sour cream are a match made in heaven. Aldean used to serve this tasty fish dish with boiled potatoes.

 2 cups sliced onion
 6 schmaltz herring fillets
 3 tbsp. butter
 ⅔ cup sour cream
 Water for boiling

Place onions in saucepan and cover with water. Bring to a boil. Drain. Cut herring into serving-sized pieces and place in a small greased casserole dish. Top with boiled onions, dot with butter, and bake for about 45 minutes, or until onions have browned. Add sour cream to dish, mix, and bake for another 10 to 15 minutes. Serves 4.

Salmon in a Package

I love making quick and easy meals. This one is so simple and delicious it should be illegal. Some people like to splash a bit of wine into the packets before closing. Feel free to experiment.

> **4 salmon steaks or fillets**
> **4 sheets of aluminum foil, about twice the**
> **size of each fillet**
> **4 tsp. butter**
> **4 tsp. dried dill weed**
> **Salt and pepper to taste**

Place fish steak or fillet in center of each piece of foil. Top each with 1 teaspoon of butter and 1 teaspoon dill weed. Wrap tightly and bake at 350 degrees for about 30 minutes (depending on size and thickness of fish). Remove from oven and place each foil packet on a serving plate. Be careful of steam when opening packages. Serves 4.

Grandma's Fish Cakes

There couldn't be a less complicated recipe than this. It was always a lazy day meal at our house, either served as is with coleslaw on the side, or as fish burgers.

> **1 can (12 oz.) tuna or salmon**
> **1 egg**
> **¼ small onion, diced**
> **¼ cup breadcrumbs**
> **¼ tsp. garlic powder**
> **Salt and pepper to taste**
> **2 tsp. butter**

Mix together all ingredients, except for butter, and form into 4 patties. Melt butter in skillet and fry cakes until brown. Serves 4.

Grandma's Sweet and Sour Fish Filets

Grandpa loved to go fishing and when he brought back the catch of the day Grandma would usually make this delicious dish. Any whitefish or salmon works just as well as trout. Using gingersnaps as a thickener and sweetener is a common practice in Jewish cooking.

> **6 trout fillets**
> **2 cups water**
> **2 onions, thinly sliced**
> **2 lemons, sliced**
> **¼ cup raisins**
> **⅓ cup brown sugar, firmly packed**
> **2 tsp. salt**
> **1 bay leaf**
> **6 gingersnaps, crushed**
> **⅓ cup vinegar**

In a saucepan combine all ingredients except for gingersnaps and vinegar, and cook over low heat for about 25 minutes. Remove fish to a platter. Add gingersnaps and vinegar to the saucepan and cook over low heat, stirring constantly until smooth. Pour over fish and serve. Serves 6.

Aldean's Kreplach

A kreplach is a dumpling in Jewish cooking, a won ton in Asian cuisine, and a ravioli to the Italians. It's a basic noodle dough, filled and either boiled or fried. They can be used in soups or served with a sauce, if desired. You can either use your favorite noodle dough recipe or Aldean's.

> **3 cups flour**
> **3 eggs, slightly beaten**
> **½ cup water**
> **1 tsp. oil**
> **¼ tsp. salt**

Mix together all ingredients in a large mixing bowl, then knead until smooth and dough pulls away from the side of the bowl. Roll out on a floured surface, cut into about 2-inch squares and fill with about 1 teaspoon of your favorite filling. Fold edges over, using a fork along the edges to make sure they are sealed tightly. Cook in boiling water until they rise to the top. Makes about 2 dozen.

MEAT FILLING

2 cups browned ground beef
1 egg
1 tbsp. minced onion
Salt and pepper to taste

Combine all ingredients; mix well.

CHEESE FILLING

2 cups hoop cheese or dry cottage cheese
3 tbsp. breadcrumbs
1 egg
2 tbsp. sour cream
Salt and pepper to taste

Combine all ingredients; mix well.

KASHA FILLING

1 cup minced onion
3 tbsp. Nyafat or butter
1½ cups cooked kasha
Pepper to taste

Brown onion in fat, then add kasha and pepper.

Betty's Tater Dogs

With six grandchildren and one great-grandchild, Betty makes a lot of what she calls "kid's dishes," but adults will like this just as well.

> **8 hot dogs**
> **2 cups cooked mashed potatoes**
> **½ lb. colby or American Cheese, sliced in**
> **thin strips**
> **1 can (8 oz.) tomato sauce**

Slice hot dogs open lengthwise, but not all the way through. Fill each dog with mashed potatoes and top with slices of cheese. Cover each dog with about 2 tablespoons tomato sauce. Place on cookie sheet and bake in the oven at 325 degrees for about 20 minutes, or until cheese melts. Serves 8.

Grandma's Hot Dogs and Baked Beans

The difference between this recipe and other hot dog and bean offerings is that Grandma sliced and fried the hot dogs before adding them to the beans. It keeps the dogs from having the same soggy texture as the beans, and also helps remove a little of the fat.

> **2 cans (16 oz. each) of favorite baked**
> **beans**
> **8 kosher hot dogs**
> **½ tsp. oil or butter**

Heat beans in a large saucepan. Slice hot dogs into bite-sized pieces. Fry them in a dry frying pan till brown. Pat dry to remove excess grease then add to bean pot. Heat together about 5 minutes. Serves 4.

Slobod's Spinach Lasagna

As I've mentioned before, Grandma was health-conscious long before it was in fashion. She would often make this spinach lasagna as a nice change from meat.

> 1 lb. lasagna noodles
> 1 large onion, chopped
> 4 cloves garlic, diced
> 2 tbsp. olive oil
> 2 packages (16 oz. each) frozen, chopped
>   spinach
> 1 jar (32 oz.) favorite pasta sauce (no meat
>   added)
> 1 can (16 oz.) diced tomatoes
> 1 egg, beaten
> 1 lb. ricotta cheese
> 1½ lbs. mozzarella cheese, sliced
> ½ cup shredded Parmesan cheese
> Salt and pepper to taste

Prepare noodles according to package directions. In a large skillet, sauté onions and garlic until onions are translucent. Add spinach, pasta sauce, and can of tomatoes. Mix well, cover, and simmer for about 15 minutes over low heat. While sauce is simmering and noodles are cooking, mix egg with ricotta cheese and set aside. Slice mozzarella and shred Parmesan, if you're using fresh. Drain noodles into a colander when done. Spread a couple of tablespoons of sauce in bottom of lasagna pan, enough to keep noodles from sticking. Cover with layer of noodles. Top noodles with dollops of ricotta. Top ricotta with spinach sauce and sprinkle on some Parmesan. Repeat layering until pan is full, ending with a layer of noodles, a bit of sauce, and lots of mozzarella on top. Bake at 350 degrees for about an hour or until lasagna is bubbly and cheese has melted and browned on the top. Remove from oven and let stand about 20 minutes before serving. Serves 8 to 10.

Tofu Stir-Fry

Tofu is so healthy and is one of those wonderful foods, like mushrooms, that soaks up flavor like a sponge. This easy stir-fry will turn tofu haters into tofu lovers.

> **1 cake (12 oz.) extra firm tofu**
> **1 tbsp. peanut oil**
> **1 package (16 oz.) favorite frozen stir-fry**
>   **blend vegetables**
> **½ cup water**
> **½ cup soy sauce**
> **¼ cup firmly packed brown sugar**
> **½ tsp. powdered ginger**
> **2 cups cooked rice, brown or white**
>   **(I prefer brown)**

Cut tofu cake into 1-inch square cubes. Heat oil in skillet and sauté tofu until lightly browned. Add frozen vegetables and gently mix well. Simmer for 2 to 3 minutes while you prepare the sauce. Combine water, soy sauce, brown sugar, and ginger together in a small bowl. Mix well until sugar is dissolved. Pour on top of tofu and vegetables. Bring to a boil, lower heat, cover, and simmer for about 5 minutes. Uncover and let simmer until the sauce has reduced by half. Serve over cooked rice. Serves 4.

After a big meal, the women would gather in the kitchen to do the dishes and chat while the men snoozed in the living room.

VEGETABLES AND SIDE DISHES

✤

Side display window of Slobod's Delicatessen.

There was no such thing in our house as a meal served without vegetables and starchy side dishes. There was usually one of each. The starches were mostly in the form of potatoes, which would be baked, mashed, boiled, scalloped, or fried. Rice was a rarity, unless rice kugel was on the menu, and a pasta side dish was usually macaroni and cheese. As if starchy side dishes weren't enough, bread always accompanied the meal. I was a constant source of irritation to Grandma at mealtime because I'd let the bread plate pass me by. With a pile of starch already on my plate, I didn't think I needed any more. "How can you possibly eat a meal without bread?" she'd ask. "Bread is the staff of life!"

As I got older, I came to realize that when she was growing up in Russia, there probably wasn't always enough food to go around to feed a large family, and they used bread as a filler. But in my lifetime, there was always plenty of food to fill up on without it. Eventually, we agreed to disagree in the big bread debate. When it came to vegetables, though, there was no need for debate, except for the time Grandma tried to pass off a bowl of mashed potatoes as something that it wasn't. They were kind of watery and really bland. I kept asking her what she had done to the potatoes to make them so distasteful, but she denied knowing what I was talking about. Said they tasted just fine to her. Stubborn little woman that she was, it took her a whole week of badgering to get her to finally admit that she had added in an equal amount of mashed turnips to the mix.

Many side dishes, like kasha and bow tie noodles, can also be eaten as a complete meal by themselves. Others, like rice kugel or sweet noodle kugel, are often served as a dessert rather than with the entrée. I'll leave it to you to decide.

George Gray's Nana's Knoedels

According to *The Weakest Link*'s host, "This is a Gray family recipe that is older than dirt. My Nana (my father's mom) was born in 1899 in St. Louis, and my dad can remember eating Knoedels as a kid back in the 1930s. Before she passed away in the late '70s, Nana wrote the recipe down for future generations. As you'll see, the directions are hilarious, and the final result will leave you stuffed and happy."

**1 loaf of white bread (stale bread
    works best)**
Salt to taste
1 cup of milk
3 eggs
4 cups of milk
3 cups all-purpose flour, sifted
3 tsp. baking powder

Cut bread into cubes. Let stand overnight, then add salt and one cup of milk to cubed bread. Let stand until milk soaks into bread cubes, and then mush cubes with a fork. If necessary, mix with hand to get a mushy consistency. Add a little more milk if necessary, but not too much because then you will have to add too much flour. Then add eggs, mix well, and then slowly add about three cups of milk, but add milk carefully and slowly—three cups might be too much for the amount of bread. Sift the flour and baking powder together and add them to the bread/salt mixture, not too fast, and work it with your hands until it has the consistency to stick together, always adding just a little of the flour. When it has sort of a biscuit-type consistency, flour your hands and make knoedel balls. Set aside on floured board or pan for about 20 minutes while boiling a large pot (4 quarts) of water, to which salt (to taste) is added. Put a few knoedels in at a time—don't crowd them. After a few minutes, stir with a fork because they might stick to the bottom, and they must rise to the top because of the baking powder in them. Boil them on medium heat for 20 minutes, then set them on top of some cooked sauerkraut, which you have cooked in another pot, until ready to serve. Serve with sauerkraut, spareribs, or a few pork chops boiled separately. Serves 4 to 6.

Deli Noodle Kugel

A kugel is a pudding, made with noodles or potatoes. This is probably the simplest of all noodle kugels, but tastes so good.

½ lb. flat egg noodles
2 eggs, beaten
3 tbsp. sugar
¼ tsp. cinnamon
¼ tsp. vanilla extract
4 tbsp. melted butter
½ cup raisins

Boil noodles according to package directions. While they are boiling, mix remaining ingredients together in a large bowl. When noodles are done, drain and add them to the bowl with wet ingredients. Mix well. Pour out into a buttered 1½ quart casserole dish and bake in oven at 400 degrees until lightly browned. Serves 4 to 6.

Kathy Levine's Killer Kugel

Kathy Levine is usually busy selling her clothing line on the Home Shopping Network, and admits that cooking in general is not the thing she does best, but kugel is one recipe she does really well! There are probably as many kugel recipes out there as there are households that make it, but this particular version is my personal favorite.

1 lb. fine egg noodles
1 lb. cottage cheese
½ lb. cream cheese, softened
1 qt. milk
6 eggs, beaten
1½ cups of sugar
2 tsp. vanilla extract
1 cup golden raisins
½ stick butter, melted
Nonstick cooking spray
Graham cracker crumbs
1 tsp. cinnamon
1 tsp. sugar

Boil noodles al dente and drain. In large bowl, mix cheeses and milk. Add noodles, eggs, sugar, vanilla, and raisins. Stir well, then add butter and stir again. Pour into nonstick pan with a touch of nonstick cooking spray spray in it. Sprinkle with graham cracker crumbs, cinnamon, and sugar. Bake at 350 degrees for 45 minutes until golden bubbly, but firm to the cut. Let cool a bit before cutting into squares and serving. This dish may be served hot or cold, for breakfast or for dinner. It's a nice change from potatoes or stuffing. If there is too much for one pan, bake the extra in muffin tins, but remember to adjust baking time down to only 15 to 20 minutes for them.

Kathy's caution: "This dish is habit-forming and VERY fattening! Do not have your cholesterol measured within twenty-four hours of consumption. Enjoy!" Serves 4 to 6.

Easy Potato Kugel

This kugel makes a nice change from regular potatoes or rice as a side dish.

1 large onion, diced
2 tbsp. butter
2 cups grated raw potatoes
2 eggs, beaten
½ cup flour
½ tsp. baking powder
1½ tsp. salt
¼ tsp. garlic powder
Pepper to taste
⅛ lb. butter

In a saucepan, sauté onion in 2 tablespoons butter until lightly browned. In a bowl, mix potatoes and eggs. Sift together dry ingredients and add to potato mixture. Stir in remaining butter and onions. Pour ingredients into greased 1-quart casserole dish and bake at 350 degrees until golden brown on top and edges are crispy (about 1 hour). Serves 4 to 6.

Rusty's Macaroni and Cheese

Mom's recipe doesn't end up like the popular creamy boxed version of mac and cheese—it's a little more rustic. In the Slobod household, we've always left it in the oven long enough for the top to get just a wee bit burnt, then all fought for the crunchy bits.

> 1 lb. pasta (Mom used whatever she had
>   on hand—elbow macaroni, penne, rotini,
>   bow ties, etc.)
> 1 lb. cheddar cheese, cut into chunks
> 1 lb. swiss cheese, cut into chunks

Boil noodles according to package directions and drain. Place in slightly greased (or sprayed with nonstick cooking spray) large casserole dish. Mix noodles with ¾ of the cheese, then sprinkle the top with remaining cheese, and bake at 350 degrees for about an hour, or until lightly browned on top. Serves 4.

Kasha with Bow Tie Noodles and Onions

Kasha is buckwheat groats. Probably an acquired taste because once you try it, you either love it or hate it. Mixing it with lots of grilled onion and pasta certainly helps the likeability factor.

> 8 oz. bow tie noodles
> 1 cup kasha
> Salt to taste
> 1 egg, beaten
> 3 cups boiling water
> 1 onion, sliced into thin rings
> 1 tbsp. oil

Cook noodles according to package directions. Set aside. Mix kasha, salt, and egg in saucepan and stir constantly until the kasha is dry and separated, or make according to package directions. Add water, cover, and simmer over low heat until all the water is absorbed. Meanwhile, sauté onion in oil until caramelized. When kasha, noodles, and onion are done, combine in a large bowl and mix well. If the mixture seems to be on the dry side, you can add a little extra oil or margarine in the final mix. Serves 6.

Grandma's Sneaky Mashed Potatoes

Every so often, in the name of healthy eating, Grandma would try and sneak something healthy into something that wasn't. In this case, she snuck some mashed turnips into the mashed potatoes. I really wasn't thrilled at her healthy mashed potatoes until I tried the recipe myself and added a couple of extra ingredients of my own.

1 lb. medium boiling potatoes
½ lb. turnips, sliced
⅓ cup milk
¼ cup softened butter or margarine
⅛ tsp. garlic powder
Salt and pepper to taste

Boil potatoes and turnips until soft. Transfer to large mixing bowl and mash together. Add milk slowly and blend to desired consistency. Add butter and seasonings, and beat until potatoes are light and fluffy. Serves 4 to 6.

Vegetable-Stuffed Potatoes

This is great as a hearty side dish, but it can also be a vegetarian meal. Using light margarine and low-fat cheese makes this a healthier, yet still tasty, offering.

2 baking potatoes
2 tbsp. butter
1 cup fresh or frozen vegetables, cooked to
    taste
½ cup favorite shredded cheese
Salt and pepper to taste

Bake potatoes in oven or microwave until done (about 1 hour at 400 degrees in the oven and about 7 minutes in the microwave. Don't forget to pierce the potatoes with a knife to avoid them exploding). When done, split potatoes in half and dot with butter (about a tablespoon for each potato). Place cooked vegetables on top of potatoes, season, and sprinkle with cheese. Put back in oven or microwave until cheese melts. Serves 2.

Judy's Potato Latkes (Potato Pancakes)

Potato latkes are a staple in any Jewish home. They can be made with flour or, on the holidays, with matzo meal. The batter can also be made ahead and refrigerated.

> **4 baking or boiling potatoes (about 1¼ lb.),**
> **peeled**
> **1 medium onion (about ½ lb.)**
> **1 egg**
> **2 tsp. chopped fresh parsley**
> **1 tsp. salt**
> **¼ tsp. white pepper**
> **2 tbsp. all-purpose flour**
> **½ tsp. baking powder**
> **½ cup vegetable oil**
> **Applesauce or sugar (powdered or**
> **granulated) for garnish**

Grate potatoes and onion, and then put them in a colander. Squeeze mixture to press out as much liquid as possible. Transfer to a bowl. Add egg, parsley, salt, white pepper, flour, and baking powder. Mix well. Heat oil in large, deep, heavy skillet. For each pancake, drop about 2 tablespoons potato mixture into pan. Flatten with back of a spoon so each cake is about 2½ to 3 inches in diameter. Fry over moderate heat about 4 to 5 minutes on each side, or until golden brown and crisp. Turn very carefully so oil doesn't splatter. Drain on paper towels. Stir potato mixture before frying each new batch. If all of the oil is absorbed, add a little more to the frying pan. Serve hot, accompanied by applesauce or sugar. Makes about 15 pancakes.

Judy's Sweet Potato and Apple Casserole

This is a terrific accompaniment to chicken, beef, or pork. The apples and sweet potatoes really complement each other well.

> **3 lb. sweet potatoes**
> **2 or 3 Granny Smith or Golden Delicious**
> **apples**
> **¼ cup freshly squeezed lemon juice**

Wash and dry sweet potatoes, then prick holes in potatoes with fork. Bake in preheated 400-degree oven for 30 to 35 minutes. Let potatoes cool, then peel and cut into quarter-inch slices. Peel and core apples, cut into eighths then ½-inch slices. Toss in a bowl with lemon juice.

MAPLE GLAZE

> **4 tbsp. butter**
> **⅓ cup firmly packed light brown sugar**
> **¼ cup maple syrup**
> **¼ tsp. cinnamon**

In saucepan, combine ingredients and stir over moderate heat until sugar dissolves. Alternate layers of sweet potatoes and apples in buttered 14-by-9-by-2-inch gratin dish. Pour glaze slowly and evenly over potato and apple mixture and bake for 25 minutes or until apples are tender. Baste frequently. Serves 6 to 8.

Easy Scalloped Potatoes

While this is the basic recipe, please feel free to be creative. I like to add grilled onions to mine.

1 pint sliced, raw potatoes
Butter for greasing baking dish
Salt and pepper to taste
1 tbsp. flour
1 tbsp. butter
1 cup scalded milk

Place layer of potatoes in bottom of buttered baking dish. Sprinkle with salt, pepper, and flour and dot with butter. Repeat layers until there are no more potatoes. Pour scalded milk over all and bake at 350 degrees for about 45 minutes. Serves 4.

Baked Broccoli, Cauliflower, and Cheese

This is another one of those easy, one-dish oven casseroles that takes very little effort to prepare, yet yields great results. This recipe calls for frozen vegetables, but you can easily use fresh. Just blanch them until slightly soft and cut into pieces.

1 bag (16 oz.) broccoli florets
1 bag (16 oz.) cauliflower
Salt and pepper to taste
2 tbsp. butter
1 lb. favorite cheese, shredded
¼ cup grated Parmesan cheese

Prepare vegetables according to package directions. Drain. Layer vegetables in baking dish, season with salt and pepper, and dot with butter. Sprinkle cheeses evenly on top and bake at 350 degrees until cheese melts and turns golden brown. Serves 4.

Jenette's Sour Cream and Beets

People just don't seem to eat enough beets. Maybe they are an acquired taste. In any case, Jenette's version couldn't be easier. She says her grandmother, Mrs. Lorincz, sometimes mixed in a few boiled potatoes as well.

1 can (16 oz.) beets
Sour cream to taste

Put beets in microwaveable dish. Place dollop of sour cream over them. Microwave on high for about 1 minute, or until heated through. Or, you can just eat them cold. Serves 2.

Slobod's Sour Cream and Mushrooms

Mushrooms are so versatile you can do just about anything with them, and the combination of mushrooms with grilled onions is heavenly. Add sour cream to the mix and you've got a wonderfully delicious side dish.

2 lb. thinly sliced mushrooms (fresh
button or crimini are best)
1 large onion, diced
4 tbsp. butter
½ tsp. garlic powder
Salt and pepper to taste
4 tsp. flour
2 cups sour cream

Sauté mushrooms and onions in butter until onions are clear and mushrooms are quite soft. Add garlic powder and season to taste with salt and pepper. Mix in flour, then cover and simmer on low for about 3 to 4 minutes. Remove to a serving dish and stir in sour cream until thoroughly blended. Serves 4 to 6.

Deli Corn Pudding

This dish works best with corn fresh off the cob, but you can used canned or frozen when fresh sweet corn isn't in season.

6 ears of corn
1 tbsp. butter
1 tbsp. flour
1 cup hot milk or half-and-half
½ tsp. sugar
Salt to taste
1 egg, beaten

Strip corn off ears and boil in a saucepan until tender. Melt butter in saucepan or in microwave in a microwaveble dish, then add flour. Mix well. Gradually stir in milk until smooth. Add seasonings, corn, and egg. Pour into buttered 2-quart baking dish and bake at 350 degrees for about half an hour or until golden brown. Serves 4 to 6.

Stuffed Tomatoes

Stuffed tomatoes make a great light side dish. Don't confuse this dish with the traditional cold tuna salad stuffed tomatoes usually served at mah-jongg parties.

6 large tomatoes
1 tbsp. chopped onion
1 tbsp. butter
1 cup seasoned breadcrumbs
Salt and pepper to taste

Slice tops off tomatoes and scoop out meat, being careful not to scoop out too much meat—you're just trying to get out the seeded part. Brown onion in butter, then add breadcrumbs, salt, and pepper. Fill tomatoes with mixture, place in a shallow baking dish, and bake in a 350-degree oven for about 30 minutes. Serves 6.

Carrot Tzimmes

Tzimmes is a side dish of cooked mixed vegetables and fruits. Carrots, peas, prunes, potatoes and sweet potatoes are the most popular ingredients. Grandma preferred the carrot, sweet potato, and apple variety. The word tzimmes literally means a fuss. Because making this side dish required a lot of preparation, it became a tzimmes.

> **3 carrots, sliced**
> **4 medium sweet potatoes, sliced**
> **3 Granny Smith apples, sliced**
> **½ cup firmly packed brown sugar**
> **Salt and pepper to taste**
> **3 tbsp. butter**
> **1 cup water**

Boil carrots and sweet potatoes until tender, then drain. Peel and core apples, then cut into quarters and slice into ¼-inch slices. Place layer of sweet potatos, then carrots, and then apples in the bottom of a 2-quart casserole dish. Cover each layer with brown sugar, salt and pepper, and dot with butter. When done layering, add water. Then cover and bake in a 350-degree oven for about half an hour, or until apples and sweet potatoes are tender. Remove cover and bake until golden brown. Serves 4 to 6.

Grandma's Honey-Glazed Carrots

So simple to make, and so yummy. This is the one side dish I most associate with Grandma because she made it often.

> **9 carrots, pared and sliced**
> **3 tbsp. butter**
> **2 tbsp. water**
> **¼ cup honey**
> **1½ tsp. salt**

Place carrots in saucepan. Add remaining ingredients. Cover and cook over low heat for 20 minutes or until carrots are tender. Stir often, but be careful not to break up carrots. Serves 4.

Grandpa's Favorite Stuffed Cucumbers

Just about any vegetable can be pared or stuffed. It's very popular in Middle Eastern cultures to stuff eggplant, okra, and squash. So why not a cucumber?

4 cucumbers
1 cup vinegar
1 cup chopped pecans
6 tbsp. mashed potatoes
1 egg, beaten
1 tsp. salt
2 bsp. chopped parsley
½ tsp. white pepper
Dash of grated nutmeg
2 tbsp. melted butter

The night before making this dish, cut the cucumbers in half lengthwise and remove the seeds with a spoon. Lay face down in vinegar overnight to marinade.

When ready to prepare, remove the cucumbers from the vinegar and wipe dry. Fill with mixture made from pecans, potatoes, egg, salt, parsley, pepper and nutmeg. Bake in a buttered baking dish until tender. Serves 4.

Joy's Hawaiian Gelatin

Hmmm. . . . I wonder what the Hawaiian phrase for very, very good is.

**2 packages (6 oz. each) lime-flavored
  gelatin
½ pint sour cream
1 jar (3 oz.) maraschino cherries,
  stems removed
1 can (16 oz.) pineapple chunks, drained
½ cup chopped walnuts (optional)**

Prepare gelatin according to package directions, but use leftover pineapple juice to replace some of the water (use all of the pineapple juice, then make up for remaining liquid needed with water). Add remaining ingredients, mix well, pour into gelatin mold, and refrigerate until firm. Serves 6.

Heart-Stopping Grebenes

Do not—I repeat—DO NOT eat grebenes more than once a year. It's pure fat and will clog your arteries faster than you can say *oy gevalt!* This is the Jewish version of the Hispanic chicharonnes, which is fried pork skin.

**1 chicken skin
1 lb. schmaltz
1 small onion, diced
¼ cup water**

Cut chicken skin into 1-inch squares. Place the skin, schmaltz, onion, and water into a large saucepan, and simmer over low heat until all the fat has been rendered and the chicken skin is crispy. Strain off the schmaltz, drain the grebenes. Some people like to use the grebenes as a topping for chopped liver while others just like them plain. Serves 4.

Secret Sauce for Vegetables

The secret of this sauce is that it is so simple to make, yet your family and friends won't have a clue as to what's in it. It tastes like it took hours to prepare, and works well on both cooked and raw vegetables. Don't scoff at its simplicity—once you try it, you'll make it all the time.

1 cup mayonnaise
1½ tbsp. soy sauce (or to taste)

Place mayonnaise in bowl and add desired amount of soy sauce. Mix well and serve. Makes 1 cup of sauce.

DESSERTS

Whether it was a birthday, anniversary, holiday, or a visit from out-of-town company, there was always an occasion for dessert.

It didn't matter that you felt like you were ready to explode after a meal at our house—it was mandatory that you ate dessert. And there was no "Go sit in the living room and let the food settle before I bring the dessert out." It was always served immediately. It was a no-win situation because if you tried to cut back on the meal to save room for dessert Grandma would complain you weren't eating enough. If you managed to eat enough and then didn't have room for dessert, she'd complain that you ate like a bird, so how could you possibly not have enough room?

Grandma couldn't understand how anyone could possibly sit at the table after a full meal, have a cup of coffee or tea, and not have a cookie or a piece of cake to go along with it. To her, that was akin to eating lox without the bagel and cream cheese, or blintzes without sour cream—it just wasn't done.

There was usually more than one dessert served at the end of each meal: fruit and a sweet. Grandma would put out a large bowl of fresh fruit and then have cookies or some kind of cake to go along with it. When strawberries were in season, we'd eat them almost every day. But instead of whipped cream or sugar on top, we'd use a dollop of sour cream instead—delicious! During the winter months, stewed, dried fruit in the form of a compote was what she liked best, and it was a nice change from the fresh apples, oranges, and pears.

As most Jewish grandmothers will constantly remind you, life is too short to skip dessert, so go on, *eppes essen.* Have a little.

Heartwarming Baked Apples

On a cold winter night, the smell of baked apples in the oven truly warms the heart and whets the appetite.

**4 Granny Smith, Rome Beauty, and/or
  Golden Delicious (or any other firm
  variety) apples
4 tbsp. brown sugar or honey
Raisins to taste
½ tsp. cinnamon
Water for bottom of baking dish**

Cut about ½-inch off top of apple and set aside. Core apples and fill each with about a teaspoon brown sugar or honey, and ¼ cup raisins, depending on taste. Sprinkle with cinnamon. Place top of apple back on and bake in a baking dish with about ¼-inch of water in the bottom of the dish at 350 degrees until apples are soft and tender when pierced with a fork. Serves 4.

Judy's Apple Crisp

A crisp is a baked dessert made with fruit. I remember first having apple crisp in my elementary school cafeteria. It was great then, and even better now.

**1 cup flour
¾ cup sugar
¼ lb. margarine
6 apples (firm variety), pared, cored, and
  sliced
½ cup water
Cinnamon (optional)**

Cream together flour, sugar, and margarine. Place apple slices into an ungreased cake pan or Pyrex dish. Add ½ cup water and sprinkle on a generous amount of cinnamon if desired. Sprinkle apples with combined mixture of flour, sugar, and margarine, then bake at 425 degrees for 45 minutes or until top browns. This is great served with vanilla ice cream! Serves 4 to 6.

Grandma's Stewed Prunes

Don't say "yuck" until you've tried them.

1 lb. unsweetened prunes
¾ cup water
½ cup sugar, or to taste

Combine ingredients in saucepan and bring to a boil. Cover and cook over low heat for about 15 minutes. Serve warm or cold. Serves 4.

Grandma's Prune Whip

Yes, another prune recipe, but don't turn up your nose. Grandma ate prunes all the time and lived to be eighty-nine.

1 lb. pitted prunes
2 egg whites
Sugar to taste
1 tbsp. confectioners' sugar

Soak prunes overnight in enough water to barely cover them. Then cook in same water until tender. Drain liquid, cool, and finely chop prunes. Sweeten to taste with sugar. Beat egg whites until firm. Add confectioners' sugar and then prunes. Mix thoroughly and refrigerate until ready to serve. Top with whipped cream, if desired. Serves 4.

Almond Cream Pudding

Grandma didn't make this very often, but it's one of those desserts everybody really looked forward to. If you're not a big almond fan, you can substitute any other flavored extract.

> 2 egg yolks
> 1½ tbsp. cornstarch
> 3 tbsp. brown sugar
> 1 pint milk, scalded
> ⅛ tsp. almond extract
> 2 egg whites
> 2 tbsp. sugar

Mix egg yolks, cornstarch, and brown sugar, then add scalded milk. Bring mixture to boil in a saucepan and stir constantly until thick. Add almond extract and mix well. Pour mixture in baking dish.

Make a meringue by beating egg whites with sugar until firm peaks are formed. Spread meringue over pudding and bake at 375 degrees until browned. Serves 4.

Grandma Hudson's Creamy Rice Pudding

There are only three words to describe this version of rice pudding: Thick, creamy, and delicious.

> 2 cups white rice
> 1 cinnamon stick, broken into large pieces
> 6 cups water
> 1 can (12 oz.) condensed milk
> 1 cup raisins
> 1 tbsp. vanilla
> 1 cup sugar

Cook rice and cinnamon stick in water until all liquid is absorbed and rice is plump and fluffy. Stir in condensed milk, raisins, vanilla, and sugar, and simmer over low heat about 3 to 5 minutes, mixing occasionally so that rice won't burn. Serves 4 to 6.

Easy Rice Pudding

While Grandma used to slave over a hot stove for most of the dishes she prepared, she'd often make rice pudding the easy way.

1 package (6 oz.) vanilla pudding
1½ cups white cooked rice
½ cup raisins, or to taste
½ tsp. cinnamon

Prepare pudding according to package directions, then add rice, raisins, and cinnamon. Refrigerate until thickened. Serves 4.

Baked Rice Pudding

There are hundreds of varieties of this tempting treat. Some are made on the stove; others, like this version, are baked. Some have apples or apricots, this one has raisins.

1 cup white rice
4 tbsp. butter or margarine
1 cup sugar
3 eggs
½ tsp. cinnamon
½ tsp. vanilla extract
1 cup raisins

Cook rice according to package directions. While rice is cooking, cream together butter and sugar, then add the rest of the ingredients and mix well. Add cooked rice to mixture and bake in greased 1-quart casserole dish at 350 degrees for about an hour. This dish can be eaten hot or cold, but it's much better slightly warm. Some people like to pour a little milk or cream over the top as well. Serves 6.

Grandma's Chocolate Pudding

There are few foods as comforting as a nice warm dish of homemade chocolate pudding.

> **1 pint milk**
> **2 tbsp. cornstarch**
> **½ cup sugar**
> **2 tbsp. grated baking chocolate**

In a large saucepan, bring milk to just boiling. Dissolve cornstarch in 2 tablespoons cold milk and add to saucepan. Add sugar and chocolate and bring to a boil until mixture thickens. Pour into serving dishes. This can either be eaten warm or refrigerated. Serves 4.

Slobod's Coconut Tapioca

Another one of those comfort foods that warms the soul as well as the stomach. This tapioca is made the old-fashioned way.

> **4 tbsp. tapioca**
> **1 qt. milk**
> **3 egg yolks**
> **⅔ cup sugar**
> **⅓ cup shredded coconut**
> **1 tsp. vanilla extract**
> **3 egg whites**
> **3 tbsp. sugar**

Soak tapioca according to package directions. The next morning, drain water and add milk; mix well. Bring mixture to a slow boil in a saucepan. Beat egg yolks with ⅔ cup sugar and add to saucepan. Cook until thickened, stirring constantly. Remove from stove and add coconut and vanilla.

Make meringue with egg whites and 3 tablespoons sugar. Spoon over tapioca and bake at 350 degrees until lightly browned. Serves 4.

Pineapple-Upside-Down Kugel

This is a variation on the standard lokchen kugel recipe. Since I love a good pineapple-upside-down cake, I figured an upside down kugel would be just as good—and it is.

½ lb. flat egg noodles, cooked
2 eggs, beaten
3 tbsp. sugar
4 tbsp. melted butter
½ tsp. vanilla extract
½ tsp. cinnamon
1 can pineapple slices, reserve juice
Pinch of salt
Maraschino cherries (one for each
    pineapple ring used)

Cook noodles according to package directions and drain. Set aside. Mix together eggs, sugar, butter, vanilla, cinnamon, reserved pineapple juice, and pinch of salt, then add noodles and mix until well-blended. Sprinkle the bottom of a greased 1½-quart baking dish with brown sugar. Place enough pineapple slices to cover bottom of pan. Fill each ring with a cherry. Top with noodle mixture and bake at 375 degrees for about an hour. Remove from oven and let cool just a bit (about 20 minutes). Then, put a serving plate on top of casserole, and invert kugel onto serving plate so that pineapple and cherries are on top. Serves 6.

Mrs. Lorincz's Apricot/Pineapple-Upside-Down Cake

Mrs. Lorincz took the standard pineapple-upside-down cake and punched it up a bit with the addition of apricots.

¼ lb. butter
1 cup brown sugar
1 can (8 or 9 oz.) apricot halves
1 can (8 oz.) pineapple, drained

Melt butter in 11-inch cast iron skillet. Add brown sugar and mix until smooth. Add apricot halves, placing face side up. Spoon drained pineapple around apricots. Set aside.

CAKE BATTER

2 egg yolks
1 cup sugar
7 tbsp. apricot juice
1 cup flour
1 tsp. baking powder
2 egg whites

Beat egg yolks. Add sugar and apricot juice. Then sift together flour and baking powder. Add to egg mixture. In a separate bowl, beat egg whites until stiff, but not dry. Fold into mixture gently. Pour over apricot mixture in skillet. Bake in skillet at 350 degrees for 30 to 40 minutes. Makes 8 to 10 servings.

Judy's Quick Banana Cake

Bananas always ripen too quickly, and banana cake is the perfect solution to use them up.

2 cups unsifted flour
1 cup sugar
1 tsp. baking soda
1 cup mashed ripe bananas
⅔ cup mayonnaise (don't use light or
   reduced-fat mayo)
¼ cup water
1½ tsp. vanilla
½ cups finely chopped walnuts

Grease 9-by-9-by-2-inch baking pan. Stir together first three ingredients.
Add next four ingredients, then beat 2 minutes with mixer at medium speed. Stir in nuts by hand. Pour into prepared pan, and bake at 350 degrees for 35 to 40 minutes, or until cake tester inserted in center comes out clean. Cool in pan. Makes 9 servings.

Rusty's Break-Your-Arm Fruitcake

A traditional holiday treat, this fruitcake is unlike the usual bitter, brick-like, indigestible fruitcakes that are immediately either tossed out or passed on to another unsuspecting relative. It's sweet, moist, and mostly fruit, not cake, so don't think of it as purely holiday fare. It's good anytime with a nice cup of tea. The only downside is in mixing the batter. It's so thick, you'll work up a sweat. It takes a lot of muscle to mix it together.

> 1½ lb. pitted dates
> 1 lb. candied pineapple chunks
> 1 lb. candied cherries
> 2 lb. walnut or pecan halves
> 2 cups sifted flour
> 2 tsp. baking powder
> ½ tsp. salt
> 4 eggs, beaten
> ½ cup dark corn syrup
> ¼ cup firmly packed brown sugar
> ¼ cup oil (any kind, except olive oil)

Grease 10-by-4-inch tube cake pan. Line with greased wax paper. Mix together fruits and nuts. Sift flour, baking powder, and salt together, then add eggs, corn syrup, sugar, and corn oil; mix well. Pour over fruit and nut mixture and mix well. Firmly pack into pan. Bake at 275 degrees for about 2 hours and 15 minutes, or until top appears dry. Cool in pan. May be baked in two 9-by-5-by-3-inch loaf pans. Serves 8 to 10.

Mrs. Lorincz's Honey Cake

Honey cake was always a delicious treat when I was a child, and even more so when Mrs. Lorincz had one baking in the oven. The wonderful aroma wafted through the walls of our duplex and made my mouth water.

> 7 egg whites
> 7 egg yolks
> 1 cup sugar
> 1 cup honey
> 1 cup hot water
> 2 tsp. coffee
> 2 tsp. baking soda
> 4 cups flour

Whip egg whites until firm and place in refrigerator until needed. Combine yolks, sugar, honey, and mix on low speed until blended. Mix hot water with coffee. Add coffee water to mixture and stir. Sift baking soda into flour. Slowly add flour to liquid mixture. Gently fold in egg whites, and bake in a greased loaf pan at 375 degrees for 1 hour. Serves 6 to 8.

Aldean's Mayonnaise Cake

In her recipe file, Aldean just had this card titled "Cake." The addition of the mayonnaise makes it wonderfully moist and delicious and, because mayonnaise is made with eggs, there is no need to add any additional eggs to the recipe.

> 2 cups flour
> 1 cup sugar
> 4 tbsp. cocoa
> ¼ tsp. salt
> 1½ tsp. baking powder
> 1½ tsp. baking soda
> 1 cup mayonnaise
> 1 cup warm water
> 1 tsp. vanilla

Preheat oven to 325 degrees. Sift together flour, sugar, cocoa, salt, and baking powder. Dissolve baking soda in warm water. Add mayonnaise, baking soda water, and vanilla to sifted ingredients and blend well. Pour into two greased 9-inch cake pans and bake for about 30 minutes, or until toothpick inserted into cake comes out dry. Frost with your favorite frosting. Serves 8.

Judy's Walnut Glory Cake

What can I say? It's glorious!

> ¾ cup flour
> 2 tsp. cinnamon
> 1 tsp. salt
> 9 egg whites
> ¾ cup sugar
> 9 egg yolks
> 2 tsp. vanilla
> ¾ cup sugar
> 2 cups finely chopped walnuts

Combine flour, cinnamon, and salt. Set aside. Beat egg whites until they form soft mounds, then gradually add ¾ cup sugar to egg whites and beat until stiff. Refrigerate. Combine egg yolks, vanilla, and remaining sugar. Beat until thick, and stir in dry ingredients. Fold batter gently into egg white mixture with 2 cups finely chopped walnuts. Pour batter into greased tube pan and bake at 350 degrees for 55 to 65 minutes. Remove from oven and invert immediately. Frost with whipped cream or a vanilla or mocha glaze. Serves 8 to 10.

VANILLA GLAZE

1 tsp. butter
1½ cups confectioners' sugar
2½ tsp. milk
⅛ tsp. salt
¼ tsp. vanilla extract

Melt butter and add to rest of ingredients. Mix until creamy. Yields about a cup.

MOCHA GLAZE

¼ tsp. instant espresso
2 tbsp. hot water
3 tbsp. unsweetend cocoa
3 tbsp. dark corn syrup
1 tbsp. coffee-flavored liqueur
1 cup confectioners' sugar

In medium bowl, combine espresso and hot water; stir until dissolved. Stir in unsweetened cocoa, dark corn syrup, and coffee-flavored liqueur until blended. Stir in confectioners' sugar until smooth. Makes about 1 cup.

Mom's Easy Cheesecake

This is not your typical cheesecake. It's a lighter alternative that doesn't require baking. Mom always used a prepared graham cracker pie crust, but make your own if you want the extra work.

> **1 prepared graham cracker pie crust**
> **8 oz. cream cheese**
> **16 oz. whipped topping**
> **1 can favorite pie filling**

Soften cream cheese. Beat cream cheese and whipped topping together with an electric mixer until well blended. Mixture should be on the thick side. Do not overbeat. Pour mixture into prepared pie shell and top with a can of your favorite pie filling. Refrigerate at least 6 hours before serving. Serves 6.

Mrs. Lorincz's Honey Torte

A torte is a layered pastry, with a filling. Linzer tortes and Sacher tortes are probably the most popular, but this honey torte is high up on the list with them.

> **3 eggs**
> **½ cup honey**
> **½ tsp. vanilla**
> **1¼ cup whole wheat pastry flour**
> **1 tsp. baking powder**
> **6 tbsp. butter or margarine, melted**
> **1 tbsp. milk**

In medium mixing bowl, blend together eggs, honey, and vanilla until creamy. In small bowl, stir together flour and baking powder. Fold into egg mixture, and then stir in butter and milk. Pour into a greased 10-inch spring form pan. Bake at 400 degrees for 15 minutes, until top is firm. While cake is baking, prepare topping.

TOPPING

½ **cup butter or margarine**
½ **cup honey**
3 **tbsp. milk**
1 **cup sliced almonds**
½ **cup flaked coconut**
½ **tsp. cinnamon**

In medium saucepan, melt butter or margarine. Add honey, milk, almonds, coconut, and cinnamon. Bring to a boil, stirring constantly. Turn off heat and let cool.

When cake is done, spread topping over hot cake, then return cake to oven for about 12 to 15 minutes longer, until brown. Let stand until set. Makes 12 servings.

Judy's Shortbread

There is nothing better with a cup of tea than shortbread, but a lot of people shy away from making it themselves because they think it's too time-consuming.

6 **oz. butter (salted or unsalted), softened**
    but not runny
⅓ **cup sugar**
1¾ **cups all-purpose flour**
¼ **cup sugar**

Cream together butter and sugar. Add flour and mix together until a ball of dough is formed. Divide mixture in half. Press dough into two 8-inch pie pans. With thumb, make indentations all around the edges of dough. With the tines of a fork prick all over inside the indentations to make a decorative pattern. Sprinkle whole pie lightly with sugar. Using a knife, cut lightly into dough the way you would if you were cutting a pie; cut about eight to twelve pie-sized pieces. Do not cut through the dough. Place on center shelf of 350-degree oven. Bake until nice and brown, approximately 25 minutes. Cut through again into 8 or 12 pieces—previous knife marks should be visible. Leave in pan and cool on wire rack. Store in airtight tin. Makes 8 or 12 pieces.

Ginny's Pretzel Gelatin

Ginny serves this on special occasions, and it is really special! She started making it in 1993 and it was a big hit with family and friends. She says it's a must for all parties. While she prefers strawberries, you can use any other berries or a different flavor of gelatin as well.

2 cups crushed pretzels
2 tsp. sugar
¾ cup butter, softened

Mix pretzels, sugar, and butter, and pat into a 9-by-13 baking dish. Bake for 8 minutes at 400 degrees. Let cool.

FILLING

8 oz. cream cheese
8 oz. whipped topping
1 cup sugar

Blend ingredients together and pour into baked pretzel crust.

TOPPING

1 box (6 oz.) strawberry gelatin
20 oz. frozen strawberries

Prepare gelatin according to package directions and mix in frozen berries. Let cool for about 10 minutes, then pour over cream cheese mixture and refrigerate for several hours until well-set. Serves 6 to 8.

Jenette's Favorite Pudding Chip Cookies

The beauty of this recipe is that you can use any flavor of pudding or chips, allowing you to make several varieties of cookies from one simple recipe.

> 2¼ cups all-purpose flour
> 1 tsp. baking soda
> ¼ cup sugar
> ¾ cup firmly packed brown sugar
> 1 pkg. (6 oz.) instant pudding mix
> 1 cup butter or margarine, softened
> 1 tsp. vanilla
> 2 eggs
> 1 pkg. (12 oz.) butterscotch, peanut
>   butter, white chocolate, or chocolate
>   chips
> 1 cup favorite chopped nuts

Sift together flour with baking soda and set aside. In large mixing bowl, combine sugars, pudding mix, butter or margarine, and vanilla. Beat until smooth and creamy. Then beat in eggs. When well blended, gradually add flour mixture, and then stir in chips and nuts. Using a teaspoon, drop batter onto ungreased baking sheets, about 2 inches apart. Bake at 375 degrees for 8 to 10 minutes. Makes about 7 dozen (depending on what size you make your cookies!).

Jenette's variations:
"I've used french vanilla pudding or chocolate pudding with good results. Also have tried a vanilla cheesecake flavor pudding. Butterscotch pudding is good with butterscotch chips. When I use chocolate pudding, I use white chocolate chips. You can add chocolate chips, too, then you will have double-chocolate-chip-pudding cookies!"

Grandma's Hazenblosen (Deep-Fried Egg Kichel)

Hazenblozen are similar to Mexican churros. They are bits of deep-fried dough, drained and sprinkled with cinnamon and sugar. It takes a while to make them, but they'll be eaten up in no time at all.

1¾ cups flour
2 eggs, beaten
Pinch of salt
2 qt. oil
Sugar and cinnamon

Mix flour, eggs, and salt into a soft dough, then roll out on lightly floured surface to about ¼-inch thickness. Cut into desired shapes and fry in oil a few at a time until golden brown. Place fried dough on paper towels to drain, then sprinkle with sugar and cinnamon. Makes about 2 dozen.

HOLIDAY DISHES

Henry carving the holiday meal.

In the kosher home, every Friday night, or Sabbath Eve, is a holiday. Traditionally, the three most important ingredients of the Sabbath meal are the *Kiddush* (prayer) wine, candles for the prayer, and a big loaf of fresh challah (egg bread). It's a holiday meal with many courses, traditionally starting with the wine, then gefilte fish and horseradish, chicken soup, brisket or roast chicken, vegetables, side dishes, dessert, and a hot beverage. In other words, the prayers nourish the soul and the meal takes care of the body. On Saturday, the Sabbath, no cooking is done because it's a day of rest, so it's a good thing you ate well the night before because cold leftovers are pretty much all you'll get.

The other major holidays are Rosh Hashana (the New Year celebration), Sukkot (the Feast of Tabernacles, which is a festival of thanksgiving), and Chanukah (the Feast of Dedication, or the Feast of Lights). Then there's Purim (a children's holiday, and the last festival before Passover), Yom Kippur (the Day of Atonement, which is a day to fast), Passover (eight days of commemorating the redemption of the children of Israel from slavery, where no *hometz,* or leaven, is eaten), and Shavuot (the harvest festival).

I remember when I was in elementary school, Passover was a week of matzo sandwiches in my lunch box. While my grandparents never kept kosher in the true sense (we didn't have a separate set of dishes for Passover), we did have a traditional Seder with all the bells and whistles the first night when my Aunt Dena and Uncle Isadore were in town. When they weren't, we skipped the ritual and just had a big family meal.

Passover is probably the most difficult holiday to cook for because of the no-leavening rule, so here are a few recipes to get you started.

Steven's Meshuggana Scramble

"This is the breakfast of Jewish champions even during the High Holy Days because it fills the kishkes before a good tennis match and a long day in *shul,*" according to Steven.

> 4 eggs, well-beaten
> 4 oz. cream cheese, softened
> 1 pinch of granulated garlic
> ⅛ tsp. dried basil
> 1 lightly toasted egg bagel
> 1 tomato slice

Combine eggs, cream cheese, garlic, and basil in blender. Blend on frappé setting for 2 minutes. Heat nonstick skillet over medium heat. Pour contents of blender into skillet, and scramble to desired doneness. Serve on lightly toasted egg bagel, topped with tomato slice. Makes 1 serving.

Gefilte Fish Shmear

So what do you do with a leftover jar of gefilte fish? Mash it up!

> 1 jar (16 oz.) gefilte fish
> ¼ cup mayonnaise
> 2 tbsp. horseradish

Mash the gefilte fish with fork and add mayonnaise and horseradish. Mix well. Serve with crackers or matzo. Serves 6.

Matzo Meal Fried Chicken

As healthy as Grandma tried to be in her cooking, she did an awful lot of frying. I guess she thought it was the ingredients and not the cooking method that made the difference.

> 2 cups matzo meal
> ¼ tsp. garlic powder
> Salt and pepper to taste
> 1 egg
> 1 tsp. water
> 1 (2 to 3 lb.) frying chicken, cut up into
>   serving-sized pieces
> Oil for frying

Mix matzo meal with seasonings and set aside. Crack an egg onto a plate and mix with water. Rinse chicken pieces, then dip into egg mixture, and roll in matzo meal mixture. Heat about ¼-inch of oil in skillet over medium heat. Cook chicken about 10 minutes until light brown. Reduce heat to low, cover, and simmer about 30 minutes, turning once or twice until chicken is thoroughly cooked. Remove cover about 5 minutes before done to ensure crispiness. Serves 4.

Vegetable Loaf

A nice change from meat, this veggie loaf is as nutritious as it is delicious.

> 1 cup chopped onion
> 2 tbsp. oil
> 1 cup chopped celery
> 1 cup grated carrots
> 1 cup finely chopped walnuts
> 1 cup matzo meal
> 1 tsp. poultry seasoning
> 1 tsp. salt
> ¼ tsp. oregano
> ¼ tsp. garlic powder
> 2 eggs
> 1 cup evaporated milk
> 1 can (10.75 oz.)cream of mushroom soup

Fry onions in oil until lightly browned. Add celery, carrots, walnuts, matzo meal, and seasonings. Sauté lightly for about 5 minutes. In separate bowl, beat eggs and stir in milk. Add mixture to pan. Simmer for couple of minutes, then allow to cool for about 10 minutes. Place mixture into greased meatloaf pan and bake at 350 degrees for about 45 minutes, or until browned. When ready to serve, prepare the mushroom soup according to can directions and use it as gravy. Serves 4 to 6.

Meatloaf *Mit* Matzo Meal

Even though you might think that this would turn out to be a very dense and heavy loaf, it's actually quite light. *(Mit* is Yiddish for "with.")

2½ lb. ground beef
1 grated onion
2 eggs
1 cup matzo meal
1 can (16 oz.) tomatoes
½ tsp. garlic powder
¼ tsp. oregano
Salt and pepper to taste

Mix together all ingredients and place in meatloaf pan. Bake for about 1 ½ hours at 350 degrees. Serves 4 to 6.

Grandpa's Marrow Dumplings

It's very trendy these days to eat marrow. It's a favorite at one New York City restaurant that caters to chefs and at other posh eateries. Grandpa was savoring these marrow dumplings long before any of those chefs were even born.

1 large marrowbone
1 egg
1 tbsp. of diced onion
1 tbsp. chicken fat
2 tbsp. fresh parsley, minced
⅛ tsp. nutmeg
½ tsp. salt
¼ tsp. garlic powder
½ cup matzo meal
Prepared chicken broth

Scoop out 2 tablespoons of marrow from the bone. Place in bowl of ice water and press marrow until all the blood can be removed and marrow is white. Then remove marrow to a mixing bowl and cream until smooth. Add egg and mix well. Sauté onion in chicken fat until just caramelized. Add onion, parsley, nutmeg, salt, and garlic powder to marrow mixture, then add matzo meal until thick, but still moist. Refrigerate for about an hour. When ready to cook, put chicken soup in saucepan, roll dumpling dough into little balls (about half the size of Ping-Pong™ balls), and drop dumplings in chicken soup. Simmer for about 15 to 20 minutes before serving. Makes about 2 dozen dumplings.

Passover Pasta Noodles

It's going to sound like a pancake at first, but this recipe really will turn out noodles—trust me. They can either be used in soup, or topped with your favorite pasta sauce. Double or triple the recipe as needed.

1 tbsp. matzo meal
2 tbsp. water
2 eggs, beaten
Pinch of salt
¼ cup flour
⅛ cup flour for dusting noodles

Combine all ingredients except for ⅛ cup flour in mixing bowl. Mix until batter is smooth. Pour a thin layer of batter into a greased 6-inch frying pan. Make sure bottom surface of pan is completely covered with batter. Cook until golden brown, then flip over and brown the other side. Repeat process until all batter is used up. Tightly roll pancakes and cut crosswise into very fine strips. Separate into noodles. Dust lightly with ⅛ cup flour and fluff to separate. Let dry a bit before using with your favorite pasta sauce or other recipe that calls for pasta noodles. Makes 1 cup of noodles.

Rusty's Corn Fritters

Corn was one of my mother's favorite vegetables and she would cook it in as many ways possible. In keeping with the holiday tradition, she used matzo meal instead of the usual flour in these fritters.

3 egg yolks, beaten
2 cups whole kernel corn, fresh or canned
¼ tsp. garlic powder
Salt and pepper to taste
¼ cup matzo meal
3 egg whites, beaten
Oil for frying

Beat egg yolks and stir in corn, seasonings, and matzo meal. Fold in beaten egg whites. Heat oil (enough to fill about ½ inch of skillet) and drop tablespoons of batter into it and fry until browned on both sides. Remove from pan and drain on paper towels before serving. Serves 6.

Passover Potato Latkes

The only difference between Passover latkes and regular latkes is that these are made with matzo meal instead of flour.

3 cups grated, raw potatoes
1 grated onion
2 eggs
¾ cup matzo meal
Salt and pepper to taste
Schmaltz or oil for frying

After grating, place potatoes in a clean tea towel and squeeze out excess moisture. Mix potatoes with onion, eggs, matzo meal, salt, and pepper. Mix well, and then drop by tablespoonful into schmaltz or oil (which should be enough to fill about a ½ inch of frying pan). Latkes should be about 2 to 3 inches in diameter. Fry until golden brown on both sides. Remove from pan and drain on paper towel. Serve with applesauce or sour cream. Makes about a dozen latkes.

Spongy Fritters

I don't know exactly why Grandma called these spongy. Maybe because the batter resembles a sponge cake batter? Who knows? The main thing is, they're delicious.

5 eggs
⅔ cup matzo meal
Pinch of salt
Oil for deep frying
Honey

Beat eggs until creamy. Add matzo meal and salt. Drop teaspoonfuls of batter into hot oil (enough to fill up about 1/2% inch of the frying pan) and fry till golden. Drain on paper towels. Serve with honey drizzled over them. Makes about 48 fritters.

Carrie's Matzo Balls

In our family, we have always scoffed at those light, fluffy matzo balls people brag about. We need to have substance in ours. My mother often joked that you wouldn't want to drop one on your foot, but they sure taste good going down. Carrie's matzo balls are not only substantial, but are substantially good!

1 dozen eggs
12 half eggshells of water
¼ butter, melted
Salt and pepper to taste
2 lb. matzo meal
Boiling water (about 3 qt.) to cook matzo
    balls

Crack eggs into a mixing bowl, reserving one solid eggshell half. Fill eggshell half 12 times with water and add to eggs. Beat well, then add melted butter. Sprinkle liquid with enough black pepper to completely cover and set aside for at least 30 minutes. Then add matzo meal, and mix well with your hands until well-blended and, according to Carrie, you can lift up the mixture in your hands and the bowl will come with it. Form mixture into balls about the size of a small orange, and drop one at a time into boiling water, and let simmer for about 30 minutes. The balls will swell when cooking, so don't cook too many at a time—maybe cook only six at a time. Because the balls will float to the top of the pan, make sure you push each one down at least twice during the cooking process. Remove with a slotted spoon and place in bowls of steaming hot chicken soup. Makes 22 to 24 matzo balls.

Slobod's Deli Matzo Kugel

In the deli, they would sweeten this kugel with apples and add chewy chopped almonds—*so* good.

> 12 matzos
> 2 apples, peeled, cored, and grated
> 2 tbsp. oil
> 4 egg yolks
> 1 tsp. cinnamon
> ⅔ cup sugar
> Pinch of salt
> ½ cup chopped almonds
> 4 egg whites, stiffly beaten

Soak matzos in water to soften and then squeeze out excess water. Place in bowl and add apples and oil. Mix egg yolks, cinnamon, sugar, and salt, and add to matzo mixture. Stir in almonds and then fold in egg whites. Pour into a large, greased casserole dish and bake for 1 hour at 325 degrees until browned. Serves 6.

Passover Blintzes

The main difference between Passover blintzes and regular blintzes is that matzo meal is used rather than flour.

> 3 eggs
> ½ tsp. salt
> ¾ cup finely sifted matzo meal
> 1½ cups water

Beat eggs, add salt, and alternate adding matzo meal and water. Mix thoroughly until you have a smooth batter. Put about 3 tablespoons of batter into a greased, hot skillet, and, like a crepe, spread batter thin to cover entire bottom of pan. Fry until brown on one side and remove.

EASY CHEESE FILLING

1 lb. cottage cheese
1 egg
1 tbsp. heavy cream
½ tsp. sugar
Pinch of salt
½ cup raisins (optional)

Mix all ingredients thoroughly. Spread blintzes with filling, fold sides, and roll up. When all blintzes are filled and rolled, fry lightly in butter until golden brown. Serves 4 to 6.

Charoseth

Charoseth is a ceremonial offering of the Seder meal that represents the bricks made and used by the Israelites when they were enslaved by Egypt. Traditionally made of fruit, nuts, and honey, there are hundreds of variations. This was Grandma's favorite way of making it.

1 apple, peeled and coarsely grated
½ cup chopped walnuts
1 tsp. honey
¼ tsp. cinnamon
1 tbsp. Manischewitz™ cherry wine
Pinch of ginger

Mix all ingredients together until smooth and lump free. Serve on matzo.

Grandma's Ingberlach

When I was a child, this sticky nut and farfel Passover candy was the thing I looked forward to the most. You don't need a lot of ingredients to make it, but you will need to use lots of elbow grease during the preparation, and lots of wet napkins for cleanup.

1 lb. honey
½ cup sugar
½ tsp. ginger
8 oz. matzo farfel
¼ cup chopped almonds

In large saucepan, bring honey, sugar, and ginger to a boil, stirring constantly. Add farfel and almonds and mix well. Continue stirring until mixture is almost too thick to stir, or candy thermometer reaches the soft-crack stage. Pour out mixture on a wet board or slab of marble, dip your hands in ice water, and flatten mixture to about ½-inch thickness. Let cool slightly, then cut into 2-inch squares with a sharp, wet knife, and transfer squares to a large platter, in single layers, and refrigerate to set.* Makes about 3 dozen squares when cut.

*When Grandma served them, she brought out the platter, and we would pry the ingberlach off the plate with a dinner knife and eat it with our fingers. It's not a dainty process, but who cares?

Teiglach

Teiglach is a baked dough dipped in a sticky sweet syrup and coated with nuts.

6 eggs
1 tbsp. oil
2½ cups cake meal
Nonstick cooking spray

Beat eggs, add oil and cake meal, and mix well to form a soft dough. Roll dough into long, thin strips with your hands on a board sprinkled with cake meal (enough to cover the board). Cut into ½-inch lengths and bake on pan sprayed with nonstick cooking spray at 350 degrees for about 10 minutes.

SYRUP

1 lb. honey
½ tsp. ginger
1 cup sugar
½ lb. chopped almonds or walnuts

Mix honey, ginger, and sugar bring to a boil in saucepan. Add nuts and dough. Boil slowly, stirring frequently. When mixture holds together when a bit is dropped on a wet surface (it should only take a few seconds to get to this point), it's done. Turn out onto a wet board and let cool until you are able to comfortably handle it with your bare hands. Wet your hands, and then shape into size of Ping-Pong™ balls.

Aldean's Passover Sponge Cake

Aldean's sponge cakes were always light and fluffy. They melted in your mouth.

6 egg yolks
Pinch of salt
Juice and rind of ½ lemon
¼ cup sugar
½ cup matzo meal, sifted
½ cup potato flour
6 egg whites
½ cup sugar

Beat together egg yolks, salt, lemon juice and rind, and ¼ cup sugar until light. Slowly add in matzo meal and potato flour. Set aside. Beat egg whites till firm, adding ½ cup sugar by the tablespoonful as egg whites thicken. Fold egg whites mixture into yolk mixture. Pour batter into greased cake pan and bake at 350 degrees for about 40 minutes.

Judy's Passover Nut Cake

What a treat!

¾ **cup matzo meal**
¾ **cup potato starch**
½ **tsp. salt**
6 egg yolks
1¾ **cups sugar**
1 cup orange juice
1½ **cups ground walnuts**
1 tbsp. grated lemon rind
6 egg whites, stiffly beaten

Mix matzo meal, potato starch, and salt together. In a separate bowl, beat egg yolks until thick and gradually add sugar, beating until lemon colored. Add matzo-meal mixture alternately with orange juice. Fold in walnuts and lemon rind, and then egg whites. Put into a 9-inch-round tube pan. Bake at 325 degrees for 1 hour or until browned and cake shrinks away from sides of pan. Cool on cake rack. Serves 6 to 8

Passover Nutty Fruity Chocolate Cake

In my humble opinion, chocolate cake should be served as often as possible. This particular cake is full of goodies.

4 egg yolks
½ **cup sugar**
¼ **lb. almonds or walnuts, finely chopped**
4 tsp. cocoa
¼ **lb. raisins**
½ **cup sifted matzo meal**
Juice of 1 orange
½ **tsp. vanilla extract**
4 egg whites

Cream egg yolks and sugar until light and creamy. Add cocoa, nuts, raisins, matzo meal, orange juice, and vanilla. Blend well. Beat the egg whites until stiff and fold into the cake mixture. Line two 8-inch cake pans* with waxed paper and pour half the mixture into each. Bake at 325 degrees until toothpick inserted into the middle of the cake comes out dry, about 15 to 20 minutes.

*You can also make this a sheet cake if you prefer. Baking time might be a little longer.

GLOSSARY

Blintz: Akin to a crepe, it's a pancake of sorts, filled with cheese or fruit filling, rolled up and then fried in butter. Blintzes are usually served with sour cream or applesauce.

Borscht: A hearty soup, made with beef, beets, or both. Classically, a borscht is served hot, but there are also wonderful cold beet borschts. Either is great served with a dollop of sour cream.

The deli counter at Henry's Los Angeles deli.

Bubbeh: A Jewish grandmother.

Charoseth: A Passover Seder offering made of fruit and nuts, representing the mortar in the bricks the Jews were forced to make when enslaved by Egypt.

Crudités: Assorted raw vegetables and fruit, cut into small pieces and served as an appetizer, sometimes with a dip or sauce.

Curaçao: A fruit-flavored liqueur.

Dollop: A measurement roughly equivalent to a heaping teaspoonful.

Fleishig: The Jewish term for meat.

Fricassee: A French term referring to meat or poultry that is browned lightly, stewed, and cooked in its own stock.

Fritter: A small cake of batter, sometimes containing corn, fruit, or some other ingredient, fried in deep fat or sautééd.

Gazpacho: A spicy cold soup made with the basic ingredients of tomatoes, cucumbers, onions, and peppers.

Gefilte fish: A traditional Jewish dish made from ground fish, especially such freshwater fish as carp, pike, or whitefish, fillets blended with eggs, matzo meal, and seasoning, shaped into balls or sticks and simmered in a vegetable broth. Similar to a quenelle in non-Jewish parlance.

Giblets: Edible internal organs of poultry including the heart, gizzard, and liver.

Golabki: Stuffed cabbage, also called halkes or praakes.

Grebenes: Chicken cracklings made by frying chicken skin in chicken fat.

Hazenblosen: Dough that has been deep-fried and then sprinkled with sugar and cinnamon. Literally means "blown-up little pants."

Hoagie buns: These are long, oval sandwich buns, sometimes also called grinder buns.

Hoop cheese: Dry curd cottage cheese.

Hors d'oeuvres: Appetizers or finger food.

Ingberlach: A traditional Passover candy made with matzo farfel, honey, ginger, and chopped almonds.

Kaiser roll: A round, crusty bread roll topped with poppy seeds.

Kasha: Buckwheat groats.

Knaidlach: Dumplings usually made of matzo meal and served in chicken soup.

Knish: A fried or baked turnover or roll of dough with a filling such as meat, kasha, cheese, or potato.

Knoedel: A flour dumpling.

Kosher: This term literally means "fit to eat," because it's clean according to the dietary laws of Judaism, and blessed by a rabbi.

Kreplach: A triangular or square dumpling, similar to ravioli or a won ton.

Kugel: A pudding, usually made with rice or noodles.

Lox: A kind of brine-cured salmon, having either a salt cure or a sugar cure, often eaten with cream cheese on a bagel.

Matzo: A flat, unleavened cracker made of flour and water.

Matzo balls: Dumplings made with matzo meal.

Matzo farfel: Small, broken-up pieces of matzo.

Matzo meal: Matzo that has been ground to a powder.

Nosh: A snack, tidbit, a bite, or a nibble.

Rokeach Nyafat™: A kosher shortening sometimes used instead of schmaltz.

It tastes like chicken fat, but isn't. It can be purchased in the kosher section of most large grocery stores.

P'cha: Calf's foot soup and jelly, depending on how you serve it.
Pfannkuchen: A large pancake.

Pickling spices: A mixture of spices used for pickling foods such as cucumbers, tomatoes, or corned beef. Usually included are allspice, bay leaves, cardamom, cloves, red and black pepper, coriander, ginger, and mustard seed.

Plotz: A slang term meaning to burst or explode.

Rouladen: Slices of meat that are flattened, filled, rolled up, and then browned in a skillet and, finally, simmered in a broth.

Saltpeter: Common name for potassium nitrate, which is commonly used as a preservative.

Schav: A cold soup made from sorrel, or sour grass.

Schmaltz: Chicken fat.

Schmaltz herring: A fatty saltwater fish. Schmaltz herring can usually only be found in a kosher store.

Schmear: To spread.

Schnapps: Intoxicating spirits. Any happy event was occasion for a toast with a schnapps.

Teiglach: A honey-nut pastry.

Torte: A rich dessert made with filled layers of cake or hard meringue.

Tzimmes: A side dish made with mixed cooked vegetables and fruit that have been slightly sweetend.

CONTRIBUTORS

Family and Friends

Lena Slobod, a.k.a. Grandma: The chief cook and matriarch of the family. Along with her husband, Henry, they owned and ran Slobod's Deli in Philadelphia. Grandma single-handedly fattened up the entire family, and in the process instilled upon me her love of family and cooking. Lena passed away in 1984 at the age of eighty-nine.

Henry Slobod, a.k.a. Grandpa: After they left the East Coast and moved to California, Grandpa managed a small deli in Los Angeles, owned his own deli for a while, then became a butcher for the Big Six Market in downtown Los Angeles. Our family was truly spoiled because Grandpa always brought home the best cuts of meat. He passed away in 1964 at the age of sixty-nine.

Rusty Brooks McKilligan, a.k.a. Mom: Henry and Lena's daughter, and my mother. Rusty, whose birth name was Evalyn, was literally raised in Slobod's Deli because the family lived in a small apartment upstairs. After the move to California, Mom didn't remain in the family business. Instead, she opted to become a private investigator. She retired to Las Vegas in 1990, and passed away in 2004 at the age of seventy-five.

Aldean Slobod: Aldean was the perfect example of not having to be Jewish or a grandmother to cook like one. When Aldean, a *shiksa,* married into the family, she embraced the Jewish culture and became a magnificent Jewish cook. Together, she and her husband, Jack, ran the other Slobod's Deli in Philadelphia, owned by Henry's brother, Pop. After the move to California, Aldean also worked as a butcher in a small Los Angeles market. Aldean passed away in 1992 at the age of eighty.

Virginia Fegley: A magnificent cook, Ginny and I have been best friends since junior high when her family moved in down the street. She still lives in southern California with her husband Steve. The Fegleys have three grown children and have recently welcomed their first grandchild. Their house is always filled with hungry family and friends.

Christina Hudson: Christina is Virginia's mother. Born in Tampico, Mexico, Christina has always had the *mi-casa-es-su-casa* ethic, and it's a good thing she did because I was always over at their house when I was a teenager. She made me feel like a member of the family, and fed me well and often. Virginia acquired all the basic skills and her love of cooking from Christina, who cooks such delicious meals that she should have opened her own restaurant. Today, she lives just a couple of blocks away from Virginia's family.

Carrie Axelrod: Carrie and I are cousins. Because she has always lived in Denver and I've always lived in Hollywood we didn't exactly grow up together, but got together every couple of years during my childhood when my grandparents and I traveled to Denver to visit their family. Carrie still lives in Denver with her husband, David, and they have two grown sons and two grandbabies.

Joy and Leon Tulper: Joy and Leon are Carrie's parents. Joy is a wonderful cook and still always cooks extra so the kids and grandkids can take a big pot of food home. Leon cooks a bit as well and the kids always flock home when he says he's going to prepare his famous pfannkuchen breakfast.

Jenette Morrison: Jenette and I have been best friends all our lives. As a baby, Jenette's grandmother, Mrs. Lorincz, often took care of her while her mother was at work. Because the Lorincz family and the Slobod family lived in the same duplex, we were literally thrown together in the cradle. Jenette lives in St. Peters, Missouri, with husband Gary and their teenage daughter, Heather.

Judy King: Judy is Jenette's mother, and the mother of two other daughters and grandmother of four. Judy learned a lot of great recipes from her own mother, Margarit Lorincz, and created a few of her own specialties throughout the years as well.

Margarit Lorincz: Mrs. Lorincz was born in Hungary and brought many of her homeland's dishes with her to the United States. She passed those delectable recipes on to her own two daughters, Judy King and Vera Lubman, and they've passed them on to subsequent generations. I always thought of her as a second grandmother because Jenette and I spent equal time in both sides of the duplex. Mrs. Lorincz passed away in 1992.

Betty Morse: Betty is a longtime friend. We met several years ago while working for the same company. Betty comes from a large family, and learned early on to cook for a small army. She has two brothers and a sister, but her mother's brother had thirteen children. Betty herself has two children, six grandchildren, and one great-grandchild. She currently lives in Pontiac, Michigan, and still enjoys cooking for her children and grandbabies.

Steven May: Cooking is not easy for Steven. His love of food comes from his wife, Nina, and his mother-in-law, Vivian. Both of them are great Jewish cooks! Hopefully daughter Arianna will follow in their footsteps. Steven always shares his leftovers with his best friends, dogs Hymie and Lulu Bell. Steven and I have been friends for many years. I was introduced to Steven by my mother when he owned Pet Limo, a limousine service for pets.

Celebrity Contributors

These famous folks were kind enough to contribute to my first celebrity cookbook and their recipes were so good, I thought I'd bring them back and offer them up again for seconds.

Stanley Ralph Ross: This award-winning writer, actor, and producer said that breakfast was his favorite meal—if it was done right. He claimed that he'd been making his tomato and egg pie for over thirty years and it always worked.

Richard Simmons: This fitness guru has devoted himself to helping people get fit and stay healthy. He has a healthy appetite for good food and his lentil salad is both good and good for you.

Dr. Ruth Westheimer: As a famed sex therapist, Dr. Ruth has been offering relationship advice for over twenty years. Going on the assumption that the way to a man's heart is through his stomach, she's created a delicious dessert as part of that therapy!

 Bobby Vinton: Bobby was happy to share his mouthwatering recipe for stuffed cabbage. Even though it's not one of those recipes that can be thrown together in a hurry, it's a princely meal from the Polish Prince.

 Kathy Levine: A former audience favorite on QVC and now reigning diva of the Home Shopping Network, not to mention a motivational speaker. Kathy says her primary message is, "Do it, try it, buy it, riot!" In regard to her recipe, maybe "fix it, try it, eat it, and forget the diet!" would be more appropriate.

 George Gray: George was the host of television's *The Weakest Link, Junkyard Wars, Todd TV,* and the *$25 Million Dollar Hoax.* He says his recipe is "a Gray family recipe that is older than dirt" passed down from his nana for future generations.

 Filthy McNasty: Filthy was a legend on the Sunset Strip during the 1970s as an entertainer and the owner of Filthy McNasty's, one of the Strip's hottest hangouts. The legend of the club continues in its current incarnation as the Viper Room, and Filthy's legendary appetite for his mother's delicious rouladen continues on as well.

 Bernie Kopell: If he weren't an actor, Bernie could easily make a living as a chef. He frequently cooks delicious meals for his wife, Catrina, and his two sons, Adam and Joshua.

Thanks to one and all for sharing.

INDEX